OSBORNE REVISE!

ACCA

F9 Financial Management

NOTES

Published by Osborne Books Limited
Unit 2
The Business Centre
Molly Millars Lane
Wokingham
Berkshire RG41 2QZ

Tel 01905 748071

Email books@osbornebooks.co.uk

Website www.osbornebooks.co.uk

Printed and bound in Great Britain.

British Library Cataloguing in Publication Data

A catalogue record for this book is available from the British Library
ISBN: 978-1-911198-30-7

CONTENTS

HOW TO USE THESE *ACCA Notes*

These *ACCA Notes* have been designed to help you to:

- **Renew** your approach to syllabus areas that might not have been clear first time around. Use them to supplement your learning and to help you to clarify details of the syllabus of which you are unsure. It is easy to look things up using the detailed index and contents page and find quickly the topic you need help with

- **Refresh** topics you have covered before but may have forgotten. If it is a while since you studied a topic which underpins a higher level subject that you now need to study, for example, use them as a refresher tool to remind yourself of what you have already learnt

- **Revise** and make the best use of your time before your examinations. Take advantage of the summarised topics, learning summaries, summary diagrams, key points, definitions and exam tips to support your revision in the critical period leading up to your real exam.

PREPARING FOR THE EXAM

To pass your exam you need an understanding of the syllabus and exam technique is vital. These *ACCA Notes* follow the syllabus with succinct coverage, offering tips on how to get the best results in the exam.

ACCA Notes – ICONS

LEARNING SUMMARY

The 'learning summary' provides details of the key learning objectives of each section of content.

DEFINITION

The 'definition' boxes highlight and explain key terms.

KEY POINT

The 'key point' boxes emphasise key points which are fundamental to your understanding of the syllabus.

Do you understand?

The 'do you understand' boxes contain short form questions which are not necessarily exam style, but which test that you have understood the core syllabus content before you progress onto exam style questions.

PAPER INFORMATION

The aim of ACCA Paper F9, Financial Management, is to develop the knowledge and skills expected of a financial manager, relating to issues affecting investment, financing, and dividend policy decisions.

SYLLABUS

A   FINANCIAL MANAGEMENT FUNCTION

1   The nature and purpose of financial management

(a)   Explain the nature and purpose of financial management. [1] **Ch. 1**

(b)   Explain the relationship between financial management and financial and management accounting. [1] **Ch. 1**

2   Financial objectives and the relationship with corporate strategy

(a)   Discuss the relationship between financial objectives, corporate objectives and corporate strategy. [2] **Ch. 1**

(b)   Identify and describe a variety of financial objectives, including [2] **Ch.1**

    (i)   shareholder wealth maximisation

    (ii)   profit maximisation

    (iii)   earnings per share growth.

3   Stakeholders and impact on corporate objectives

(a)   Identify the range of stakeholders and their objectives [2] **Ch.1**

(b)   Discuss the possible conflict between stakeholder objectives [2] **Ch. 1**

(c)   Discuss the role of management in meeting stakeholder objectives, including the application of agency theory [2] **Ch. 1**

(d)   Describe and apply ways of measuring achievement of corporate objectives including [2] **Ch. 19**

    (i)   ratio analysis using appropriate ratios such as return on capital employed, return on equity, earnings per share and dividend per share

    (ii)   changes in dividends and share prices as part of total shareholder return.

(e)   Explain ways to encourage the achievement of stakeholder objectives, including [2] **Ch. 1**

    (i)   managerial reward schemes such as share options and performance related pay

    (ii)   regulatory requirements such as corporate governance codes of best practice and stock exchange listing regulations

4   Financial and other objectives in not-for-profit organisations

(a)   Discuss the impact of not-for-profit status on financial and other objectives. [2] **Ch. 1**

(b)   Discuss the nature and importance of Value for Money as an objective in not-for-profit organisations [2] **Ch. 1**

(c)   Discuss ways of measuring the achievement of objectives in not-for-profit organisations [2] **Ch. 1**

B   FINANCIAL MANAGEMENT ENVIRONMENT

1   The economic environment for business

(a)   Identify and explain the main macroeconomic policy targets[1] **Ch. 11**

(b)   Define and discuss the role of fiscal, monetary, interest rate and exchange rate policies in achieving macroeconomic policy targets[1] **Ch. 11**

(c)   Explain how government economic policy interacts with planning and decision-making in business[2] **Ch. 11**

(d)   Explain the need for and the interaction with planning and decision-making in business of[1] **Ch. 11**

   (i)   competition policy

   (ii)   government assistance for business

   (iii) green policies

   (iv)   corporate governance regulation[2]

2   The nature and role of financial markets and institutions

(a)   Identify the nature and role of money and capital markets, both nationally and internationally. [2] **Ch. 12**

(b)   Explain the role of financial intermediaries.[1] **Ch. 12**

(c)   Explain the functions of a stock market and a corporate bond market [2] **Ch. 12**

(d)   Explain the nature and features of different securities in relation to the risk/return trade-off. [2] **Ch. 15**

3   The nature and role of the money market

(a)   Describe the role of the money markets in:[1] **Ch.12/13/14**

   (i)   Providing short-term liquidity to industry and the public sector

   (ii)   Providing short-term trade finance

   (iii) Allowing an organisation to manage its exposure to foreign currency risk and interest rate risk

(b)   Explain the role of banks and other financial institutions in the operation of the money markets. [2] **Ch. 12**

(c)   Explain the characteristics and role of the principal money market instruments:[2] **Ch. 12**

   (i)   Interest-bearing instruments

   (ii)   Discount instruments

   (iii) Derivative products.

C   WORKING CAPITAL MANAGEMENT

1   The nature, elements and importance of working capital

(a)   Describe the nature of working capital and identify its elements[1] **Ch. 7**

(b)   Identify the objectives of working capital management in terms of liquidity and profitability, and discuss the conflict between them.[2] **Ch. 7**

(c)   Discuss the central role of working capital management in financial management.[2] **Ch. 7**

2   **Management of inventories, accounts receivable, accounts payable and cash**

(a)   Explain the cash operating cycle and the role of accounts payable and receivable.[2] **Ch. 7**

(b)   Explain and apply relevant accounting ratios, including: [2] **Ch. 7**

   (i)   current ratio and quick ratio

   (ii)   inventory turnover ratio, average collection period and average payable period

   (iii)   sales revenue/net working capital ratio.

(c)   Discuss, apply and evaluate the use of relevant techniques in managing inventory, including the Economic Order Quantity model and Just-in-Time techniques [2] **Ch. 8**

(d)   Discuss, apply and evaluate the use of relevant techniques in managing accounts receivable, including: **Ch. 9**

   (i)   assessing creditworthiness[1]

   (ii)   managing accounts receivable[1]

   (iii)   collecting amounts owing[1]

   (iv)   offering early settlement discounts[2]

   (v)   using factoring and invoice discounting[2]

   (vi)   managing foreign accounts receivable.[2]

(e)   Discuss and apply the use of relevant techniques in managing accounts payable, including: **Ch 9**

   (i)   using trade credit effectively[1]

   (ii)   evaluating the benefits of discounts for early settlement and bulk purchase[2]

   (iii)   managing foreign accounts payable.[1]

(f)   Explain the various reasons for holding cash, and discuss and apply the use of relevant techniques in managing cash, including: [2] **Ch. 10**

   (i)   preparing cash flow forecasts to determine future cash flows and cash balances

   (ii)   assessing the benefits of centralised treasury management and cash control

   (iii)   cash management models, such as the Baumol model and the Miller-Orr model

   (iv)   investing short-term

3   **Determining working capital needs and funding strategies**

(a)   Calculate the level of working capital investment in current assets and discuss the key factors determining this level, including: [2] **Ch.7**

   (i)   the length of the working capital cycle and terms of trade

   (ii)   an organisation's policy on the level of investment in current assets

   (iii)   the industry in which the organisation operates.

(b)   Describe and discuss the key factors in determining working capital funding strategies, including: [2] **Ch.7**

   (i)   the distinction between permanent and fluctuating current assets

   (ii)   the relative cost and risk of short-term and long-term finance

   (iii)   the matching principle

(iv)	the relative costs and benefits of aggressive, conservative and matching funding policies management attitudes to risk, previous funding decisions and organisation size.[1]
(v)	management attitudes to risk, previous funding decisions and organisation size: [1]

D   INVESTMENT APPRAISAL

1   Investment appraisal process techniques

(a)   Identify and calculate relevant cash flows for investment projects. [2] **Ch.2**

(b)   Calculate payback period and discuss the usefulness of payback as an investment appraisal method.[2] **Ch.2**

(c)   Calculate return on capital employed (accounting rate of return) and discuss its usefulness as an investment appraisal method.[2] **Ch.2**

(d)   Calculate net present value and discuss its usefulness as an investment appraisal method.[2] **Ch.3**

(e)   Calculate internal rate of return and discuss its usefulness as an investment appraisal method.[2] **Ch.3**

(f)   Discuss the superiority of DCF methods over non-DCF methods.[2] **Ch.3**

(g)   Discuss the relative merits of NPV and IRR. 2] **Ch. 3**

(h)   Calculate discounted payback and discuss its usefulness as an investment appraisal method.[2] **Ch. 6**

2   Allowing for inflation and taxation in DCF

(a)   Apply and discuss the real-terms and nominal-terms approaches to investment appraisal. 2] **Ch.4**

(b)   Calculate the taxation effects of relevant cash flows, including the tax benefits of tax-allowable depreciation and the tax liabilities of taxable profit. [2] **Ch.4**

(c)   Calculate and apply before- and after-tax discount rates.[2] **Ch.17**

3   Adjusting for risk and uncertainty in investment appraisal

(a)   Describe and discuss the difference between risk and uncertainty in relation to probabilities and increasing project life. [2] **Ch.6**

(b)   Apply sensitivity analysis to investment projects and discuss the usefulness of sensitivity analysis in assisting investment decisions.[2] **Ch.6**

(c)   Apply probability analysis to investment projects and discuss the usefulness of probability analysis in assisting investment decisions.[2] **Ch.6**

(d)   Apply and discuss other techniques of adjusting for risk and uncertainty in investment appraisal, including: **Ch.6**

    (i)   simulation[1]

    (ii)   adjusted payback[1]

    (iii)   risk-adjusted discount rates.[2]

4 **Specific investment decisions (Lease or buy, asset replacement, capital rationing, etc.)**

(a) Evaluate leasing and borrowing to buy using the before-and after-tax costs of debt.[2] **Ch.5**

(b) Evaluate asset replacement decisions using equivalent annual cost.[2] **Ch.5**

(c) Evaluate investment decisions under single-period capital rationing, including:[2] **Ch.5**

    (i) the calculation of profitability indexes for divisible investment projects

    (ii) the calculation of the NPV of combinations of non-divisible investment projects

    (iii) a discussion of the reasons for capital rationing.

E **BUSINESS FINANCE**

1 **Sources of and raising business finance**

(a) Identify and discuss the range of short-term sources of finance available to businesses, including:[2] **Ch.15**

    (i) overdraft

    (ii) short-term loan

    (iii) trade credit

    (iv) lease finance.

(b) Identify and discuss the range of long-term sources of finance available to businesses, including:[2] **Ch.15**

    (i) equity finance

    (ii) debt finance

    (iii) lease finance

    (iv) venture capital.

(c) Identify and discuss methods of raising equity finance, including:[2] **Ch.15**

    (i) rights issue

    (ii) placing

    (iii) public offer

    (iv) stock exchange listing.

(d) Identify and discuss methods of raising short and long term Islamic finance including:[1] **Ch.15**

    (i) major difference between Islamic finance and other forms of business finance

    (ii) The concept of Riba (interest) and how returns are made by Islamic financial securities

    (iii) Islamic financial instruments available to businesses including

    (iv) murabaha (trade credit)

    (v) Ijara (lease finance)

    (vi) mudaraba (equity finance)

    (vii) sukuk (debt finance)

    (viii) musharaka (venture capital) (note calculations are not required)

(e)   Identify and discuss internal sources of finance, including: [2] **Ch.15**

    (i)   retained earnings

    (ii)   increasing working capital management efficiency.

    (iii)   the relationship between the dividend decision and the financing decision[2] **Ch.16**

    (iv)   the theoretical approaches to, and the practical influences on, the dividend decision, including legal constraints, liquidity, shareholding expectations and alternatives to cash dividends[2] **Ch.16**

2   Estimating the cost of capital

(a)   Estimate the cost of equity, including:[2] **Ch.17**

    (i)   Application of the dividend growth model and discussion of its weaknesses

    (ii)   Explanation and discussion of systematic and unsystematic risk

    (iii)   Relationship between portfolio theory and the capital asset pricing model (CAPM)

    (iv)   Application of the CAPM, its assumptions, advantages and disadvantages.

(b)   Estimating the cost of debt [2] **Ch.17**

    (i)   irredeemable debt

    (ii)   redeemable debt

    (iii)   convertible debt

    (iv)   preference shares

    (v)   bank debt.

(c)   Estimating the overall cost of capital, including:[2] **Ch.17**

    (i)   Distinguishing between average and marginal cost of capital

    (ii)   Calculating the weighted average cost of capital (WACC) using book value and market value weightings.

3   Sources of finance and their relative costs

(a)   Describe the relative risk-return relationship and the relative costs of equity and debt [2] **Ch.17**

(b)   Describe the creditor hierarchy and its connection with the relative costs of sources of finance.[2] **Ch.17**

(c)   Identify and discuss the problem of high levels of gearing.[2] **Ch.18**

(d)   Assess the impact of sources of finance on financial position, financial risk and shareholder wealth using appropriate measures, including: **Ch.19**

    (i)   ratio analysis using statement of financial position gearing, operational and financial gearing, interest coverage ratio and other relevant ratios[2]

    (ii)   cash flow forecasting[2]

    (iii)   leasing or borrowing to buy.[2]

(e)   Impact of cost of capital on investments, including: [2] **Ch.17**

    (i)   the relationship between company value and cost of capital

    (ii)   the circumstances under which WACC can be used in investment appraisal

    (iii)   the advantages of the CAPM over WACC in determining a project-specific cost of capital

    (iv)   application of CAPM in calculating a project specific discount rate.

4   Capital structure theories and practical considerations

(a)   Describe the traditional view of capital structure and its assumptions. [2] **Ch.18**

(b)   Describe the views of Miller and Modigliani on capital structure, both without and with corporate taxation, and their assumptions. [2] Ch.**18**

(c)   Identify a range of capital market imperfections and describe their impact on the views of Miller and Modigliani on capital structure.[2] **Ch.18**

(d)   Explain the relevance of pecking order theory to the selection of sources of finance.[1] **Ch.18**

5   Finance for small and medium-sized entities (SMEs)

(a)   Describe the financing needs of small businesses.[2] **Ch.15**

(b)   Describe the nature of the financing problem for small businesses in terms of the funding gap, the maturity gap and inadequate security.[2] **Ch.15**

(c)   Explain measures that may be taken to ease the financing problems of SMEs, including the responses of government departments and financial institutions.[1] **Ch.15**

(d)   Identify appropriate sources of finance for SMEs and evaluate the financial impact of different sources of finance on SMEs.[2] **Ch.15**

F   BUSINESS VALUATIONS

1   Nature and purpose of the valuation of business and financial assets

(a)   Identify and discuss reasons for valuing businesses and financial assets. [2] **Ch.20**

(b)   Identify information requirements for valuation and discuss the limitations of different types of information.[2] **Ch.20**

2   Models for the valuation of shares

(a)   Asset-based valuation models, including:[2] **Ch.20**

    (i)   net book value (statement of financial position basis).

    (ii)   net realisable value basis.

    (iii)   net replacement cost basis.

(b)   Income-based valuation models, including:[2] **Ch.20**

    (i)   price/earnings ratio method

    (ii)   earnings yield method

(c)   Cash flow-based valuation models, including:[2] **Ch.20**

    (i)   dividend valuation model and the dividend growth model

    (ii)   discounted cash flow basis.

3   The valuation of debt and other financial assets

(a)   Apply appropriate valuation methods to:[2] **Ch.20**

   (i)   irredeemable debt

   (ii)   redeemable debt

   (iii)   convertible debt

   (iv)   preference shares.

4   Efficient market hypothesis (EMH) and practical considerations in the valuation of shares

(a)   Distinguish between and discuss weak form efficiency, semi-strong form efficiency and strong form efficiency.[2] **Ch.20**

(b)   Discuss practical considerations in the valuation of shares and businesses, including: [2] **Ch.20**

   (i)   marketability and liquidity of shares

   (ii)   availability and sources of information

   (iii)   market imperfections and pricing anomalies

   (iv)   market capitalisation.

(c)   Describe the significance of investor speculation and the explanations of investor decisions offered by behavioural finance.[1] **Ch.20**

G   RISK MANAGEMENT

1   The nature and types of risk and approaches to risk management

(a)   Describe and discuss different types of foreign currency risk:[2] **Ch.13**

   (i)   translation risk

   (ii)   transaction risk

   (iii)   economic risk.

(b)   Describe and discuss different types of interest rate risk: [1] **Ch.14**

   (i)   gap exposure

   (ii)   basis risk

2   Causes of exchange rate differences and interest rate fluctuations

(a)   Describe the causes of exchange rate fluctuations, including: **Ch.13**

   (i)   balance of payments[1]

   (ii)   purchasing power parity theory[2]

   (iii)   interest rate parity theory[2]

   (iv)   four-way equivalence.[2]

(b)   Forecast exchange rates using:[2] **Ch.13**

   (i)   purchasing power parity

   (ii)   interest rate parity.

(c)   Describe the causes of interest rate fluctuations, including: [2] **Ch.14**

   (i)   structure of interest rates and yield curves

   (ii)   expectations theory

   (iii)   liquidity preference theory

   (iv)   market segmentation.

3   Hedging techniques for foreign currency risk

(a)   Discuss and apply traditional methods of foreign currency risk management, including: **Ch.13**

   (i)   currency of invoice[1]

   (ii)   netting and matching[2]

   (iii)   leading and lagging[2]

   (iv)   forward exchange contracts[2]

   (v)   money market hedging[2]

   (vi)   asset and liability management.[1]

(b)   Compare and evaluate traditional methods of foreign currency risk management.[2] **Ch.13**

(c)   Identify the main types of foreign currency derivates used to hedge foreign currency risk and explain how they are used in hedging.[1] (No numerical questions will be set on this topic) **Ch.13**

4   Hedging techniques for interest rate risk

(a)   Discuss and apply traditional methods of interest rate risk management, including: **Ch.14**

   (i)   matching and smoothing[1]

   (ii)   asset and liability management[1]

   (iii)   forward rate agreements.[2]

(b)   Identify the main types of interest rate derivates used to hedge interest rate risk and explain how they are used in hedging.[1] (No numerical questions will be set on this topic) **Ch.14**

The superscript numbers in square brackets indicate the intellectual depth at which the subject area could be assessed within the examination. Level 1 (knowledge and comprehension) broadly equates with the Knowledge module, Level 2 (application and analysis) with the Skills module and Level 3 (synthesis and evaluation) to the Professional level. However, lower level skills can continue to be assessed as you progress through each module and

FORMULAE AND TABLES

Economic order quantity

$$= \sqrt{\frac{2C_oD}{C_H}}$$

Miller-Orr Model

$$\text{Return point} = \text{Lower limit} + (\frac{1}{3} \times \text{spread})$$

$$\text{Spread} = 3\left(\frac{\frac{3}{4} \times \text{Transaction cost} \times \text{Variance of cash flows}}{\text{Interest rate}}\right)^{\frac{1}{3}}$$

The Capital Asset Pricing Model

$$E(r)_j = R_f + \beta_j (E(r_m) - R_f)$$

The asset beta formula

$$\beta_a = \left(\frac{V_e}{(V_e + V_d(1-T))}\ \beta_e\right) + \left(\frac{V_d(1-T)}{(V_e + V_d(1-T))}\ \beta_d\right)$$

The Growth Model

$$P_0 = \frac{D_0(1+g)}{(r_e - g)} \qquad r_e = \frac{D_0(1+g)}{(P_0)} + g$$

Gordon's growth approximation

$$g = br_e$$

The weighted average cost of capital

$$\text{WACC} = \left(\frac{V_e}{V_e + V_d}\right)k_e + \left(\frac{V_d}{V_e + V_d}\right)k_d(1-T)$$

The Fisher formula

$$(1 + i) = (1 + r)(1 + h)$$

Purchasing power parity and interest rate parity

$$S_1 = S_0 \times \frac{(1+h_c)}{(1+h_b)} \qquad F_0 = S_0 \times \frac{(1+i_c)}{(1+i_b)}$$

Present Value Table

Present value of 1 i.e. $(1 + r)^{-n}$

Where   r = discount rate
           n = number of periods until payment

Periods   *Discount rates (r)*

(n)	1%	2%	3%	4%	5%	6%	7%	8%	9%	10%	
1	0.990	0.980	0.971	0.962	0.952	0.943	0.935	0.926	0.917	0.909	1
2	0.980	0.961	0.943	0.925	0.907	0.890	0.873	0.857	0.842	0.826	2
3	0.971	0.942	0.915	0.889	0.864	0.840	0.816	0.794	0.772	0.751	3
4	0.961	0.924	0.888	0.855	0.823	0.792	0.763	0.735	0.708	0.683	4
5	0.951	0.906	0.863	0.822	0.784	0.747	0.713	0.681	0.650	0.621	5
6	0.942	0.888	0.837	0.790	0.746	0.705	0.666	0.630	0.596	0.564	6
7	0.933	0.871	0.813	0.760	0.711	0.665	0.623	0.583	0.547	0.513	7
8	0.923	0.853	0.789	0.731	0.677	0.627	0.582	0.540	0.502	0.467	8
9	0.914	0.837	0.766	0.703	0.645	0.592	0.544	0.500	0.460	0.424	9
10	0.905	0.820	0.744	0.676	0.614	0.558	0.508	0.463	0.422	0.386	10
11	0.896	0.804	0.722	0.650	0.585	0.527	0.475	0.429	0.388	0.350	11
12	0.887	0.788	0.701	0.625	0.557	0.497	0.444	0.397	0.356	0.319	12
13	0.879	0.773	0.681	0.601	0.530	0.469	0.415	0.368	0.326	0.290	13
14	0.870	0.758	0.661	0.577	0.505	0.442	0.388	0.340	0.299	0.263	14
15	0.861	0.743	0.642	0.555	0.481	0.417	0.362	0.315	0.275	0.239	15

(n)	11%	12%	13%	14%	15%	16%	17%	18%	19%	20%	
1	0.901	0.893	0.885	0.877	0.870	0.862	0.855	0.847	0.840	0.833	1
2	0.812	0.797	0.783	0.769	0.756	0.743	0.731	0.718	0.706	0.694	2
3	0.731	0.712	0.693	0.675	0.658	0.641	0.624	0.609	0.593	0.579	3
4	0.659	0.636	0.613	0.592	0.572	0.552	0.534	0.516	0.499	0.482	4
5	0.593	0.567	0.543	0.519	0.497	0.476	0.456	0.437	0.419	0.402	5
6	0.535	0.507	0.480	0.456	0.432	0.410	0.390	0.370	0.352	0.335	6
7	0.482	0.452	0.425	0.400	0.376	0.354	0.333	0.314	0.296	0.279	7
8	0.434	0.404	0.376	0.351	0.327	0.305	0.285	0.266	0.249	0.233	8
9	0.391	0.361	0.333	0.308	0.284	0.263	0.243	0.225	0.209	0.194	9
10	0.352	0.322	0.295	0.270	0.247	0.227	0.208	0.191	0.176	0.162	10
11	0.317	0.287	0.261	0.237	0.215	0.195	0.178	0.162	0.148	0.135	11
12	0.286	0.257	0.231	0.208	0.187	0.168	0.152	0.137	0.124	0.112	12
13	0.258	0.229	0.204	0.182	0.163	0.145	0.130	0.116	0.104	0.093	13
14	0.232	0.205	0.181	0.160	0.141	0.125	0.111	0.099	0.088	0.078	14
15	0.209	0.183	0.160	0.140	0.123	0.108	0.095	0.084	0.074	0.065	15

Annuity Table

Present value of an annuity of 1 i.e. $\dfrac{1-(1+r)^{-n}}{r}$

Where   r = discount rate

         n = number of periods

Periods   *Discount rates (r)*

(n)	1%	2%	3%	4%	5%	6%	7%	8%	9%	10%	
1	0.990	0.980	0.971	0.962	0.952	0.943	0.935	0.926	0.917	0.909	1
2	1.970	1.942	1.913	1.886	1.859	1.833	1.808	1.783	1.759	1.736	2
3	2.941	2.884	2.829	2.775	2.723	2.673	2.624	2.577	2.531	2.487	3
4	3.902	3.808	3.717	3.630	3.546	3.465	3.387	3.312	3.240	3.170	4
5	4.853	4.713	4.580	4.452	4.329	4.212	4.100	3.993	3.890	3.791	5
6	5.795	5.601	5.417	5.242	5.076	4.917	4.767	4.623	4.486	4.355	6
7	6.728	6.472	6.230	6.002	5.786	5.582	5.389	5.206	5.033	4.868	7
8	7.652	7.325	7.020	6.733	6.463	6.210	5.971	5.747	5.535	5.335	8
9	8.566	8.162	7.786	7.435	7.108	6.802	6.515	6.247	5.995	5.759	9
10	9.471	8.983	8.530	8.111	7.722	7.360	7.024	6.710	6.418	6.145	10
11	10.37	9.787	9.253	8.760	8.306	7.887	7.499	7.139	6.805	6.495	11
12	11.26	10.58	9.954	9.385	8.863	8.384	7.943	7.536	7.161	6.814	12
13	12.13	11.35	10.63	9.986	9.394	8.853	8.358	7.904	7.487	7.103	13
14	13.00	12.11	11.30	10.56	9.899	9.295	8.745	8.244	7.786	7.367	14
15	13.87	12.85	11.94	11.12	10.38	9.712	9.108	8.559	8.061	7.606	15

(n)	11%	12%	13%	14%	15%	16%	17%	18%	19%	20%	
1	0.901	0.893	0.885	0.877	0.870	0.862	0.855	0.847	0.840	0.833	1
2	1.713	1.690	1.668	1.647	1.626	1.605	1.585	1.566	1.547	1.528	2
3	2.444	2.402	2.361	2.322	2.283	2.246	2.210	2.174	2.140	2.106	3
4	3.102	3.037	2.974	2.914	2.855	2.798	2.743	2.690	2.639	2.589	4
5	3.696	3.605	3.517	3.433	3.352	3.274	3.199	3.127	3.058	2.991	5
6	4.231	4.111	3.998	3.889	3.784	3.685	3.589	3.498	3.410	3.326	6
7	4.712	4.564	4.423	4.288	4.160	4.039	3.922	3.812	3.706	3.605	7
8	5.146	4.968	4.799	4.639	4.487	4.344	4.207	4.078	3.954	3.837	8
9	5.537	5.328	5.132	4.946	4.772	4.607	4.451	4.303	4.163	4.031	9
10	5.889	5.650	5.426	5.216	5.019	4.833	4.659	4.494	4.339	4.192	10
11	6.207	5.938	5.687	5.453	5.234	5.029	4.836	4.656	4.486	4.327	11
12	6.492	6.194	5.918	5.660	5.421	5.197	4.988	4.793	4.611	4.439	12
13	6.750	6.424	6.122	5.842	5.583	5.342	5.118	4.910	4.715	4.533	13
14	6.982	6.628	6.302	6.002	5.724	5.468	5.229	5.008	4.802	4.611	14
15	7.191	6.811	6.462	6.142	5.847	5.575	5.324	5.092	4.876	4.675	15

TOP 10 TIPS TO IMPROVE YOUR RESULT

Be organised and plan your study time – there are more tips on how to do this below.

'Mens sana in corpore sano' – prepare your body; sleep well and eat right as a healthy body leads to a healthy mind!

Study according to your learning style – different people have different learning styles. Some people are visual learners, some people prefer sound, some need physical motion – try out different methods to see what works best for you.

Try using a study buddy – this could be someone taking the same exam, or a friend or family member.

Revise knowledge efficiently – stay focused, stop procrastinating and don't let your mind wander.

Read questions very carefully – many students fail to answer the actual question set. Read the question once right through and then again more slowly. Make note of key words in the question when you read through it.

Ensure you know the structure of the exam – how many questions (and of what type) you will be expected to answer. During your revision, attempt all the different styles of questions you may be asked.

Be a good test-taker. Get lots of practice – the ACCA release sample assessments and practice CBE mock exams are available.

Read good newspapers and professional journals, especially ACCA's *Student Accountant* – this can give you a distinct advantage in the exam.

Adopt a positive mental attitude. You may have nerves and feel anxious but with the correct preparation and practice you can have confidence in your ability to succeed.

PLAN YOUR STUDY TIME

Decide which times of the week you will devote to revising.

Put the times you plan to revise onto a study plan for the weeks from now until the exam and set yourself targets for each period of revision, ensuring that you cover the whole syllabus.

If you are studying for more than one paper at a time, try to mix and match your subjects as this can help you to keep motivated and see each subject in its broader context.

When working through your course, compare your progress with your plan and, if you fall behind, re-plan your work (perhaps including extra sessions). If you are ahead, do some extra revision/practice questions.

EXTRA QUESTIONS

Practising exam standard questions is a critical part of your revision.

Specimen Exams and Practice Tests are available from
http://www.accaglobal.com/gb/en/student/exam-support-resources.html

and Exam Kits and Mock Exams in the style of the real exam can be obtained from

http://kaplan-publishing.kaplan.co.uk/acca-books/pages/acca-books.aspx.

1 The financial management function

The following topics are covered in this chapter:

- The nature and purpose of financial management
- Corporate strategy and financial objectives
- Stakeholder objectives and conflicts and the role of management
- Not for profit organisations

1.1 THE NATURE AND PURPOSE OF FINANCIAL MANAGEMENT

LEARNING SUMMARY

After studying this section you should be able to:

- explain the nature and purpose of financial management
- explain the relationship between financial management and financial and management accounting

KEY POINT Financial management is concerned with acquiring and using financial resources in both the short and long term, to ensure the objectives of an enterprise are achieved.

Financial management decisions involve three key areas:

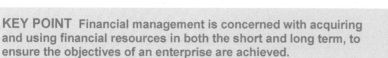

Investment – both long-term investment in non-current assets and short-term investment in working capital

- **investment appraisal** considers the **long-term** plans and identifies the right projects to adopt
- **working capital management** is concerned with the **short-term**, i.e. the management of liquidity

Finance – from what sources should funds be raised?

Identification of the most **appropriate sources** (both long and short-term)

Dividends – how should cash funds be allocated to shareholders and how will the value of the business be affected by this?

Making decisions on:
- whether to **return** any cash to the owners in the form of **dividends**, or
- **retaining** some or all of the cash for **reinvestment**

The three key areas will consider:

- the organisation's **commercial and financial objectives**
- the broader **economic environment**
- the potential **risks**.

An understanding of these three key areas is fundamental for the exam

Financial roles

KEY POINT Financial management should be distinguished from other important financial roles.

Management accounting	Providing information for the **day to day** functions of **control and decision making**, for example overhead apportionment and variance analysis
Financial accounting	Providing information about the **historical** results of an organisation for **owners and other stakeholders**, for example calculating depreciation and identifying accruals
Financial management	The **long term** raising of **finance** and the **allocation and control** of **resources**, for example examining the proposed expansion plans of a business

1.2 CORPORATE STRATEGY AND FINANCIAL OBJECTIVES

LEARNING SUMMARY

After studying this section you should be able to:

- discuss the relationship between financial objectives, corporate objectives and corporate strategy
- identify and describe a variety of financial objectives

KEY POINT Objectives and targets define what an organisation is trying to achieve. Strategy considers how.

Corporate objectives – the overall mission of an organisation is broken down into commercial goals

⟶ These are set by the top-level management of an organisation.
For example, to improve the brand awareness.

Corporate strategy – how the corporate objectives will be achieved

⟶ Senior managers will decide how to achieve the corporate objectives.
For example, entering a new market.

Financial objectives – the objectives of an organisation that can be measured in monetary terms

⟶ For example, to improve profitability by 5% compared to the previous year

---

Corporate strategy decisions and financial objectives are set at the top of an organisation and are **filtered down** to ensure all parts of an organisation are working to achieve the same goal:

- **business level** – the overall organisation split into separate business units
- **operational level** – the day-to-day operations of business units

Financial objectives

KEY POINT A fundamental financial objective of an organisation is the maximisation of shareholder wealth. The three key decisions (investment, finance and dividends) should be adhered to when considering this objective.

Shareholder wealth maximisation – the primary objective of most organisations is to increase the net worth of its shareholders

This can be achieved by increasing the share price and/or a dividend pay-out.

Profit maximisation – the ability of an organisation to achieve the maximum profit with minimum expenditure

There may be a conflict between long and short-term goals. For example, cutting discretionary spending may increase short term profits but have a negative impact long term.

Earnings per share (EPS) growth – earnings per share is profit divided by the number of shares and growth shows how it has increased over a period of time

The disadvantage is that it does not represent the income of the shareholder.

When examining financial objectives, a distinction must be made between **maximising** and **satisficing.**

DEFINITION **Maximising** - seeking the maximum level of returns, even though this might involve exposure to risk and much higher management workloads.

DEFINITION **Satisficing** - finding a merely adequate outcome, holding returns at a satisfactory level, avoiding risky ventures and reducing workloads.

For example, an organisation might seek to **maximise** the **return for shareholders** and **satisfy** the **requirements of employees.**

Do you understand?

1   The financial manager of an organisation will make the following three decisions:

    A   investment, economic, dividends

    B   investment, finance, dividends

    C   economic, finance, investment.

2   Implementing a just in time (JIT) inventory system is a financial objective?

    Yes or No

3   The purchase of three new machines for £300,000 each is:

    A   a business level financial objective

    B   a business level strategy

    C   a corporate level strategy.

3   B. The purchase of the machines is a business level strategy, i.e. how an objective can be achieved.

2   No. Implementing a JIT system is a strategy (at operational level)

1   B. The three key areas a financial manager will make decisions on are investment, finance and dividends

1.3 STAKEHOLDER OBJECTIVES AND CONFLICTS AND THE ROLE OF MANAGEMENT

LEARNING SUMMARY

After studying this section you should be able to:

- identify the range of stakeholders and their objectives
- discuss the possible conflict between stakeholder objectives
- discuss the role of management in meeting stakeholder objectives
- understand and apply agency theory
- explain ways to encourage the achievement of stakeholder objectives

Stakeholders are wide ranging groups with a vested interest in an organisation, they may be internal, external, or connected to the organisation. Management must balance the needs and objectives of all stakeholders to avoid conflict as **each group are focused on furthering their own interests.** Stakeholders include:

Internal:	
Employees	maximising employee salaries will result in lower returns for investors
Managers / directors	may follow their own aims and goals, at the expenses of other stakeholders, for example short term profits to achieve higher bonuses
Connected:	
Equity investors	the primary objective of an organisation is the maximisation of shareholder wealth and it must compete with risk free investment opportunities such as government securities which investors could turn to if they are not satisfied
Customers	satisfaction of customer needs is achieved through value for money products, this could be at the expense of profit
Suppliers	need reassuring that they will be paid in the short term and retain regular business in the long term
Finance providers	the primary interest is the repayment of debt and interest in both the long and short term and they prefer low risk policies to ensure payments are made
External:	
Government	political interests include increasing exports, financial interests include maximising taxation
The community	environmental expectations of the community at large include the consideration of fuel emissions, their legal and social responsibility expectations are, for example employee welfare

The role of management

Management are uniquely placed to pursue their own interests rather than those of the shareholders, as they are usually left alone on a day to day basis.Examples include:

- Setting their own levels of **remuneration**

- **Empire building**

- **Creative accounting,** such as not depreciating non-current assets

- **Off balance sheet financing,** where the method of funding is not recorded in the balance sheet

- Defending the organisation against **takeover bids**

- Carrying out **unethical activities.**

Problems can be resolved by achieving goal conguence.

Achieving stakeholder objectives

Ways to help ensure that managers take decisions which are consistent with the objectives of stakeholders are:

Managerial reward schemes are one way of helping to ensure that managers take decisions which are consistent with the objectives of shareholders. They must be carefully designed to encourage goal congruence.

Examples include:
- Remuneration linked to **minimum profit levels**
- Remuneration linked **to economic value added (EVA),** the increase in the value of shareholder wealth in a period
- Remuneration linked to **revenue growth**
- **Executive share option scheme (ESOP),** this encourages managers to maximise the value of shares

A set of voluntary principles called **corporate governance codes** have been established to address director and shareholder conflicts.

The issues addressed include:
- At least half of the members of the board should be independent, **non-executive directors** (excluding the chair)
- The role of the **chair and chief executive officer** should be **separate**
- **Remuneration** of the **chair** and **highest paid director** should be disclosed
- **Executive directors** should submit themselves for **re-election** every three years
- There should be **independent remuneration and nomination committees**
- Shareholders should be able to **vote** separately on each **substantially separate issue**

Stock exchange listing requirements for corporate governance:

- listed companies **must** disclose how they have **applied the principles** and **complied with the code**, and
- state and explain any **deviation** from the **recommended practice**, and
- disclose full details of **directors' remuneration** packages, which should be submitted to **shareholders** for **approval.**

Do you understand?

1 Customers are an internal stakeholder of an organisation.

True or False

2 The agency problem is a driving force behind the growing importance attached to sound corporate governance. In this case the managers are the agents.

Yes or No

1.4 OBJECTIVES IN NOT FOR PROFIT ORGANISATIONS

LEARNING SUMMARY

After studying this section you should be able to:

- discuss the impact of not for profit status on financial and other objectives
- discuss the nature and importance of value for money as an objective in not for profit organisations
- discuss ways of measuring the achievement of objectives in not for profit organisations

KEY POINT The primary objective of not for profit organisations is not to make money but to benefit prescribed groups of people

Not for profit organisations include charities, public services, local government, trade unions, sports associations and professional institutes.

Objectives of not for profit organisations

Not for profit organisations will use a mixture of financial and non-financial objectives. What those objectives are will depend on:

- in whose interests is the organisation run?
- what are the objectives of the interested parties?

Financial objectives – a not for profit organisation will often have limited funds and therefore set financial targets.	Examples include: • Total amount to be **raised** • Amount to be spent on **fund raising** • Spending on **specified projects** and **administration** • **Budgetary control** • **Breakeven**

Many key non- financial objectives are difficult to quantitfy and therefore most public bodies operate under objectives determined by the government.

Value for money (VFM)

DEFINITION **Value for money –** achieving the desired level and quality of service at the most economical cost

Many not for profit organisations are funded by the public purse and the lack of clear financial performance measures can be seen as a problem.

Asessing whether an organisation provides value for money involves looking at all functioning aspects of the not for profit organisation, the three E's:

> Use of the three E's as a performance measure and a way to assess VFM, is a key issue for exam questions relating to not for profit and public sector organisations

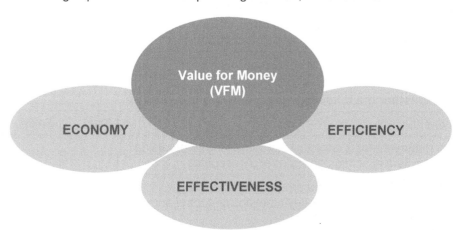

- **economy** – minimising the costs of inputs required to achieve a defined level of output, for example materials and staff

- **efficiency** – achieving a high level of output in relation to the resources put in (input driven) or providing a particular level of service at a reasonable input cost (output driven)

- **effectiveness** – whether outputs are achieved that match the predetermined objectives, i.e. the targets

Do you understand?

1   In the context of managing performance in not for profit organisations, which of the following is correct:

   A   Economy means doing things cheaply, not spending £2 when the same item can be bought for £1

   B   Efficiency means doing things quickly, minimising the amount of time spent on a given activity

1   In relation to the financial management of a company, which of the following provides the best definition of a firm's primary financial objective?

   A   To achieve long-term growth in earnings

   B   To maximise the level of annual dividends

   C   To maximise the wealth of its ordinary shareholder

   D   To maximise the level of annual profits

2   Indicate whether the following objectives are financial or non-financial objectives of a company.

Objective	Financial	Non-financial
Maximisation of market share		
Earnings growth		
Sales revenue growth		
Achieving a target level of customer satisfaction		
Achieving a target level of return on capital employed		

3   Indicate whether the following statements are true or false.

Statement	True	False
Financial management is concerned with the long-term raising of finance and the allocation and control of resources.		
Management accounting is concerned with providing information for the more day-to-day functions of control and decision making.		
Financial accounting is concerned with providing information about the historical results of past plans and decisions		

4   What is the main purpose of corporate governance?

   A   To separate ownership and management control of organisations

   B   To maximise shareholder value

   C   To facilitate effective management of organisations and to make organisations more visibly accountable to a wider range of stakeholders

   D   To ensure that regulatory frameworks are adhered to

5   Managerial reward schemes should help ensure managers take decisions which are consistent with the objectives of shareholders.

   Which THREE of the following are characteristics of a carefully designed remuneration package?

   A   Linking of rewards to changes in shareholder wealth

   B   Matching of managers' time horizons to shareholders' time horizons

   C   Possibility of manipulation by managers

   D   Encouragement for managers to adopt the same attitudes to risk as shareholders

2 Basic investment appraisal

The following topics are covered in this chapter:

- The investment appraisal process
- Return on capital employed
- Accounting profits and cash flows
- Payback

2.1 THE INVESTMENT APPRAISAL PROCESS

LEARNING SUMMARY

After studying this section you should be able to:

- define business organisations and explain why they are formed
- understand what investment appraisal means.

Capital investment is spending resources on non-current assets.

KEY POINT Investment appraisal is used to select appropriate capital expenditure projects.

Investment appraisal involves:

- assessing the level of **expected returns** earned for the level of **expenditure made**
- estimating future costs and benefits over a project's life

> Exam questions may ask you to compare and contrast the two basic techniques – return on capital employed and payback.

2.2 RETURN ON CAPITAL EMPLOYED (ROCE)

LEARNING SUMMARY

After studying this section you should be able to:

- calculate return on capital employed
- discuss its usefulness as an investment appraisal method.

A formula is used to calculate the return on capital employed percentage. It is also known as the accounting rate of return (ARR) and can be calculated in two ways:

ROCE using **initial capital costs** =

$$\frac{\text{Average annual profits before interest and tax}}{\text{Initial capital costs}}$$

The initial capital cost is the investment at the start of a project

ROCE using **average capital investment** =

$$\frac{\text{Average annual profits before interest and tax}}{\text{Average capital investment}}$$

The average capital investment = (initial investment + any scrap value at the end of the project) ÷ 2

The initial investment could include:

- costs of new assets
- net book value of existing assets
- working capital
- capitalised research and development expenditure

For example, a project will run for five years with the following information:

In the exam use the initial capital cost unless you are told otherwise. However, the average capital investment method is the one most commonly used in questions.

- initial purchase of plant - $110,000

- annual cash flows of $24,400, starting in year 1

- scrap value at the end of the project - $10,000

- depreciation is calculated on a straight line basis and therefore would be $20,000 per annum (($110,000 - $10,000) ÷ 5).

The return on capital employed using the two methods is:

initial capital costs = 4%
$$\frac{(\$24{,}400 - \$20{,}000)}{\$110{,}000}$$

Depreciation of $20,000 is deducted from the annual cash flows of $24,400 to calculate the average profit before interest and tax

average capital investment = 7.33%
$$\frac{(\$24{,}400 - \$20{,}000)}{\$60{,}000}$$

The average capital investment = ($110,000 + $10,000) ÷ 2

KEY POINT If the expected ROCE is greater than the target (set by management) the project should be accepted.

You may be asked to discuss the features of ROCE in addition to calculations.

Advantages of ROCE	Disadvantages of ROCE
Easy to calculate, based on widely reported measures of returns (profit) and asset values	It fails to take into account either the **project life** or **timing of cash flows**
ROCE is **easily understood** as it is expressed as a percentage	The ROCE figures for identical projects may vary from business to business if they use **different accounting policies** (such as depreciation) and the **decision** to invest or not is **subjective**
	Both **working capital requirements** and the **absolute gain** in wealth for the shareholders are **ignored**

Do you understand?

1   A seven year project requires an initial investment of $800,000 and at the end of the project the assets initially purchased will be sold for $100,000. The project's average capital investment is:

A $800,000

B $400,000

C $450,000

D $100,000

1 C. The initial investment plus the scrap value divided by 2. ($800,000 + $100,000) ÷ 2.

2.3 ACCOUNTING PROFITS AND CASH FLOWS

LEARNING SUMMARY

After studying this section you should be able to:

- identify and calculate relevant cash flows for investment projects.

The major differences in cash and profit are:

- asset purchase and depreciation

- deferred taxation

- changes in working capital

- capitalisation of research and development expenditure

Cash flows are a **better** measure than **profit** of the suitability of a capital investment because:

cash is what **ultimately counts**	Profits are only a guide to cash availability, they cannot be spent
profit measure is **subjective**	The time periods in which income and expenses are recorded for example are a matter of judgement
cash is used to pay **dividends**	The ultimate method of transferring wealth to shareholders

Relevant costs

KEY POINT For all methods of investment appraisal (except ROCE), only relevant costs should be considered

Relevant costs are cash flows that will happen in the future and will only arise if the capital project goes ahead.	Costs that are ignored are: • **Sunk costs** – costs that have already been incurred • **Committed costs** – costs that will be incurred anyway, for example fixed costs • **Non cash** items, for example depreciation • **Allocated costs** – these are overheads that would be incurred anyway

Do you understand?

1   A company is evaluating a proposed project with expenditure on an item of equipment that would cost $160,000. A technical feasibility study has been carried out by consultants at a cost of $15,000 into the benefits of investing in the equipment. The $15,000 is a:

   A   Relevant cost

   B   Capital cost

   C   Sunk cost

1 C. The cost has already been incurred, therefore it is sunk.

2.4 PAYBACK

LEARNING SUMMARY

After studying this section you should be able to:

- calculate the payback period

- discuss its usefulness as an investment appraisal method.

KEY POINT The payback period is the time a project will take to pay back the money spent on it. It is based on expected cash flows and provides a measure of liquidity.

Payback using **constant annual cash flows** =
$$\frac{\text{Initial investment}}{\text{Annual cash flow}}$$

For example, the payback of a seven year project with an initial investment of $1.8 million and annual cash inflows of $350,000 is 5.1 years or 5 years and 2 months.

$1,800,000 ÷ $350,000 = 5.1429

NB. To express in months (0.1429 x 12) = 2 (rounded up)

Where cash flows are uneven the payback is calculated by working out the cumulative cash flow over the life of the project, for example:

Year	Cash Flow ($000)	Cumulative Cash Flow ($000)	
0	(1,900)	(1,900)	
1	300	(1,600)	$(1,900,000) + $300,000
2	500	(1,100)	$(1,600,000) + $500,000
3	600	**(500)**	
4	800	300	**$(500,000) ÷ $800,000 = 0.625**
5	500	800	

In the exam it is important that you can discuss the features of payback as well as being able to carry out calculations.

The project is paid back somewhere between years 3 and 4. Therefore take the cumulative cash flow for year 3 and the cash flow for year 4 to perform the calculation shown above. It is 0.625 of a year or expressed in months (0.625 x 12) = 8 (rounded up), therefore 3 years and 8 months.

KEY POINT Only select projects which pay back within a specified time. If choosing between more than one project select the one with the quickest payback.

Advantages of Payback	Disadvantages of Payback
Simplicity – easy to calculate and understand	**Cash flows** arising **after** the **payback** period are **ignored**
It **favours** projects with a **quick return**, as rapid payback leads to rapid growth, minimises risk and maximises liquidity	The **time value of money** is **ignored**
For a project with **rapidly changing technology** a quick payback is essential	There is **no objective measure** as to what length of time should be set as a minimum payback period
Payback uses **cash flows** not profits	It takes **no account** of the effects of business **profits** and the periodic performance of the project

Do you understand?

1 Which of the following is an advantage of the payback method of investment appraisal?

    A   It takes account of the timing of the cash flows within the payback period

    B   It uses cash flows rather than accounting profits

    C   It takes account of the cash flows after the end of the payback period

2 Which of the following statements is false?

    (i)   The payback method of investment appraisal takes into account the length of the project

    (ii)   Focus on an early payback period can enhance liquidity

    (iii)   Investment risk is increased if the payback period is longer

1   B. Payback uses cash flows not profits.

2   (i)   Payback does not take into account the length of the project.

1   It has been estimated that the annual profits of a project would be $8,000, after deducting an annual depreciation charge of $40,000 and $25,000 for a share of an existing fixed cost. The annual relevant cash flow is:

   A $8,000

   B $73,000

   C $48,000

2   The following information relates to an investment project which is being evaluated by the directors of Fence Co, a listed company. The initial investment, payable at the start of the first year of operation, is $3.9 million.

Year	1	2	3	4
Net operating cash flow ($000)	1,200	1,500	1,600	1,580
Scrap value ($000)				100

   (a)   What is the payback period of the investment project?

       A   2.75 years

       B   1.50 years

       C   2.65 years

       D   1.55 years

   (b)   Based on the average investment method, what is the return on capital employed of the investment project?

       A   13.3%

       B   26.0%

       C   52.0%

       D   73.5%

3 Discounted cash flow techniques

The following topics are covered in this chapter:
- Net present value
- Internal rate of return

3.1 NET PRESENT VALUE

LEARNING SUMMARY

After studying this section you should be able to:

- calculate net present value and discuss its usefulness as an investment appraisal method
- discuss the relative merits and superiority of net present value.

KEY POINT Money received or paid today is worth more than the same sum received or paid in the future, it has a time value. Discounted cashflow techniques take account of the time value of money when appraising investments and projects.

Compounding – calculates the future value of a given sum invested today for a particular time period at a particular rate of interest

$$F = P (1 + r)^n$$

F = Future value   P = Initial investment (present value)

r = Interest rate   n= number of periods

for example, an investment of $500 today earns 5% interest per annum, the value after three years is:

$$F = \$500 \times 1.05^3$$

$$= \$578.81$$

Discounting – calculates the present value of an amount received or paid in the future

$$P = F (1 + r)^{-n}$$

P = Initial investment (present value)   F = Future value

n= number of periods   r = Interest rate

for example, the present value of $65,000 receivable in six years' time at an interest rate of 7% is

$$P = \$65,000 \times 1.07^{-6}$$

$$= \$43,312$$

Alternative terms for interest: cost of capital, discount rate, required return

KEY POINT Net present value (NPV) is the difference between the present value of cash inflows and outflows. If the NPV is positive the project is financially viable. For decisions between two or more projects, choose the one with the highest NPV.

An example of calculating the net present value is:

Year	Cash flow ($)	Discount factors (8%)	Present value	
0	(25,000)	1.000	(25,000)	(25,000) × 1.000
1	10,000	0.926	9,260	10,000 × 0.926
2	9,000	0.857	7,713	9,000 × 0.857
3	8,000	0.794	6,352	8,000 × 0.794
4	5,000	0.735	3,675	5,000 × 0.735
Net present value			2,000	

> Unless told otherwise, all cash flows occur at the start or end of a year and the initial investments at time period 0.

> Discount factors will be provided in the exam.

Advantages of NPV	Disadvantages of NPV
considers the time value of money	difficult to explain to managers
is an absolute ($) measure of return	requires knowledge of the cost of capital
based on cash flows not profits	relatively complex
considers whole life of project	
should lead to maximisation of shareholder wealth	

Annuities and perpetuities

An annuity is a constant annual cash flow for a number of years. A perpetuity is an annual cash flow that occurs forever:

Present value(PV) of an annuity

= annual cash flow × annuity factor (AF)

$$AF = \frac{1 - (1 + r)^{-n}}{r}$$

for example, a payment of $5,800 is to be made every year for 15 years, the first payment occurring in one year's time, the interest rate is 12%. The present value of the annuity is:

$$AF = (1 - 1.12^{-15})/12$$
$$= 6.810864489$$

PV = $5,800 × 6.810864489 = $39,503

if the tables are used = $5,800 × 6.811= $39,504

> Annuity factors will be provided in the exam.

Present value(PV) of a perpetuity

= annual cash flow × perpetuity factor

perpetuity factor = 1/r

growing perpetuity factor = 1/(r − g)

g = growth

for example, a payment of $5,800 is to be made every year for the foreseeable future, the first payment occurring in one year's time, the interest rate is 12%.

The present value of the perpetuity if the annuity remains constant is:

PV = $5,800 × 1/0.12 = $48,333

The present value of the perpetuity if there is growth of 3% from the second year is:

PV = $5,800 × 1/(0.12 − 0.03) = $64,444

if the cash flow starts at t0 this is known as an advanced annuity or perpetuity:	if the cash flow starts at a time period later than t1 this is known as a delayed annuity or delayed perpetuity:
Step 1 ignore the t0 cash flow completely	Step 1 apply the appropriate annuity/perpetuity factor to the cash flows as usual
Step 2 add one to the discount factor (for the remaining cash flows) before multiplying by the cash flow value	Step 2 discount the single cash flow back to t0 using the appropriate discount factor
for example, 3 annual payments of $5,000 starting from today at a discount rate of 10%:	**for example, 3 annual payments of $5,000 starting in 4 years at a discount rate of 10%:**
use the annuity factor for 2 years and add 1 to its value	**use the 3 year annuity factor to discount to a single sum as at t3, then use the 3 year discount factor to discount the single sum back to t0**
$5,000 × (1 + 1.736) = $13,680	$5,000 × 2.487 × 0.751 = $9,339

3.2 INTERNAL RATE OF RETURN

LEARNING SUMMARY

After studying this section you should be able to:

- calculate internal rate of return and discuss its usefulness as an investment appraisal method

- discuss the relative merits and superiority of internal rate of return.

KEY POINT The internal rate of return (IRR) is the discount rate at which the net present value is zero, it therefore represents a breakeven cost of capital. Projects should be accepted if the IRR is greater than the cost of capital.

Internal rate of return is calculated using linear interpolation:

calculate two NPVs for a project at different costs of capital

use the formula to find the IRR

$$IRR = L + \frac{N_L}{N_L - N_H}(H - L)$$

L	=	lower discount rate
H	=	higher discount rate
NL	=	NPV at the lower discount rate
NH	=	NPV at the higher discount rate.

Remember to check if an NPV is negative.

Advantages of IRR	Disadvantages of IRR
considers the time value of money	does not measure absolute profitability
is a relative (%) measure and easily understood	linear interpolation is only as estimate
based on cash flows not profits	relatively complex
considers whole life of project	non-conventional cash flows can lead to multiple IRRs
should lead to maximisation of shareholder wealth	

Do you understand?

1 Company Y has made an investment with a net present value of $42,000 at 10% and ($22,000) at 20%.

What is the internal rate of return of the project?

A   31.0%

B   16.6%

C   15.0%

D   13.4%

KEY POINT NPV and IRR are both superior DCF techniques for evaluating investment opportunities but they can give a different decision about a project. If the two measures conflict, NPV should be used as it gives the absolute increase in shareholder wealth at the business's current funding level, as represented by the cost of capital.

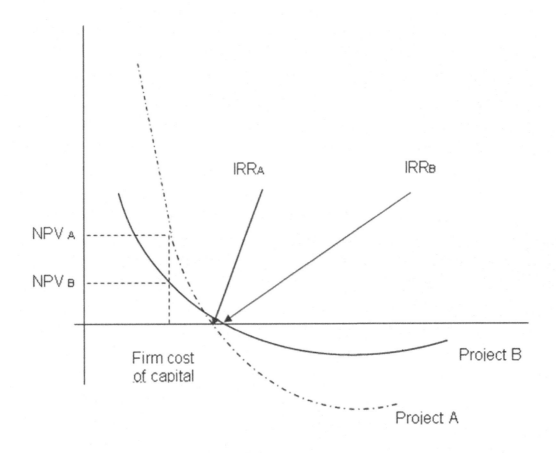

Do you understand?

1 Which of the following statements about net present value (NPV) and internal rate of return (IRR) methods are correct?

   (1) An investment with a positive NPV is financially viable

   (2) NPV is a superior method of investment appraisal compared to IRR

   (3) The graph of NPV against discount rate has a negative slope for most projects

   (4) NPV is the present value of expected future net cash receipts less the cost of investment

   A   (1) and (4)

   B   (2) and (3)

   C   (1), (2) and (4)

   D   All of them

1   **A company is considering a project which has an initial outflow followed by several years of cash inflows, with a cash outflow in the final year.**

   How many internal rates of return could there be for this project?

   A   Either zero or two

   B   Either one or two

   C   Zero, one or two

   D   Only two

2   **A project consists of a series of cash outflows in the first few years followed by a series of positive cash inflows. The total cash inflows exceed the total cash outflows. The project was originally evaluated assuming a zero rate of inflation.**

   If the project were re-evaluated on the assumption that the cash flows were subject to a positive rate of inflation, what would be the effect on the payback period and the internal rate of return?

Method	Increase	Decrease
Payback period		
Internal rate of return		

3   **Company Q wishes to undertake a project requiring an investment of $732,000 which will generate equal annual inflows of $146,400 in perpetuity.**

   If the first inflow from the investment is a year after the initial investment, what is the IRR of the project?

   A   20%

   B   25%

   C   400%

   D   500%

4   **Which THREE of the following are advantages of the IRR?**

   A   Considers the whole life of the project

   B   Uses cash flows not profits

   C   It is a measure of absolute return

   D   It considers the time value of money

Discounted cash flow further aspects

4.1 THE IMPACT OF INFLATION

LEARNING SUMMARY

After studying this section you should be able to:

- apply and discuss the real-terms and nominal-terms approaches to investment appraisal.

KEY POINT Inflation is a general increase in prices leading to a general decline in the real value of money.

In times of inflation, funding providers will require a return made up of two elements:

a real return for the use of their funds (i.e. the return they would want if there were no inflation in the economy)	an additional return to compensate for inflation (so that they don't lose out from the effects of inflation)

the overall return required from these two elements is called the money or nominal rate of return

the real and money (nominal) returns are linked by the formula:

$$(1 + i) = (1 + r)(1 + h)$$

r = real rate of return   h = inflation rate

i = money cost of capital (the company's normal cost of capital)

for example, an investor requires a real return on their investment of 12%, but in addition will need to be compensated for anticipated inflation of 3%.

the money rate of return required by the investor is:

$$(1 + i) = (1 + r)(1 + h)$$

$$r = 0.12, h = 0.03$$

$$1 + i = 1.12 \times 1.03 = 1.1536$$

$$i = 0.1536 \text{ or } 15.36\%$$

The impact of inflation on cash flows

- cash flows that have not been increased for expected inflation are described as being in current prices or today's prices

- cash flows that have been increased to take account of inflation are known as money cash flows (or nominal cash flows), they represent the expected cash outflow or inflow to hit the bank account.

> Assume in the exam that cash flows are money cash flows unless stated otherwise.

Methods of dealing with inflation:

Real method

do NOT inflate the cash flows

leave them in current terms i.e. in today's (t0) prices – current cash flows

discount using the **real rate**

$(1 + i) = (1+r)(1 + h)$

for example:
an investment costs $20,000,
expected net cash flows from the investment are $7,000 per annum in current terms and will last for four years, the cash flows are expected to be subject to inflation of 4%.
The money cost of capital for discounting is 14%

the net present value (NPV) is:

real cost of capital = (1.14/1.04) – 1 = 0.096 or 9.6%
uninflated cash flows act as an annuity for 4 years

4 year annuity factor for 9.6%:
$(1 – 1.096^{-4})/0.096 = 3.198$

NPV = (20,000) + (7,000 × 3.198) = $2,386

Money/nominal method

inflate each cash flow by its specific inflation rate i.e. convert it to a money cash flow

discount using the **money rate**

using the example above:

the NPV is:

Time	Cash flow ($)	Discount factor (14%)	Present value ($)
t0	(20,000)	1.000	(20,000)
t1	7,280	0.877	6,385
t2	7,571	0.769	5,822
t3	7,874	0.675	5,315
t4	8,189	0.592	4,848
NPV			2,370

inflated cash flows:
t1 cash flow = $7,000 × 1.04 = $7,280
t2 cash flow = $7,280 × 1.04 = $7,571

Do you understand?

1   A company has a money cost of capital of 16.55% per annum. The real cost of capital is 11% per annum.

What is the inflation rate?

A   5.00%

B   5.55%

C   11.00%

D   16.55%

4.2 DEALING WITH TAX AND WORKING CAPITAL

LEARNING SUMMARY

After studying this section you should be able to:

- calculate the taxation effects of relevant cash flows, including the tax benefits of tax-allowable depreciation and the tax liabilities of taxable profit

- understand working capital requirements.

The impact of taxation on cash flows

Assumption are:

tax inflows and outflows are relevant cash flows for NPV purposes

operating cash inflows will be taxed at the prevailing tax rate

operating cash outflows will be tax deductible and save tax at the prevailing rate

investment spending will attract tax-allowable depreciation

the business is making net profits overall

tax is paid one year after the related operating cash flow is earned

> Assume in the exam that these assumptions apply, unless stated otherwise.

Tax effects in investment appraisal:

Tax on operating cash flows ....▶
additional income = additional tax paid

additional costs = less tax paid

Tax relief on investment spending ..▶

tax-allowable depreciation is allowed as an expense against profits INSTEAD of depreciation:

- it is calculated based on the written down value of the assets (reducing balance or straight line according to the question)

- the total amount of tax-allowable depreciation given over the life of an asset will equate to its fall in value over the period (cost less scrap proceeds)

- claim as early as possible

- given for every year of ownership of the asset except the year of disposal (the tax-allowable depreciation is allowed against profits and therefore reduces the tax bill – shown as an inflow of tax on the NPV)

- in the year of disposal a balancing allowance or charge arises instead (tax equivalent of profit or loss on disposal and allowed against profits)

- timing of asset purchase is important, unless stated otherwise: first day of an accounting period – first tax-allowable depreciation claimed one year later and tax saved one year after that last day of an accounting period – first tax-allowable depreciation claimed immediately and tax saved in one year's time.

> Assume unless told otherwise in the question that the asset was purchased on the first day of an accounting period.

For example, an asset is bought for a project at a cost of $25,000 and will be used for four years before being disposed of for $5,000. Tax-allowable depreciation is available at 25% reducing balance and the tax rate is 30%.

The tax allowable depreciation and hence the tax savings for each year if tax is paid (and saved) a year in arrears is:

Year		$	Tax rate (30%) $	I year in arrears	
0	asset purchase	25,000			
1	1st tax-allowable depreciation (at 25%)	(6,250)	1,875	2	25,000 × 25%
	tax written down value	18,750			25,000 − 6,250
2	2nd tax-allowable depreciation (at 25%)	(4,688)	1,406	3	18,750 × 25%
	tax written down value	14,062			18,750 − 4,688
3	3rd tax-allowable depreciation (at 25%)	(3,516)	1,055	4	14,062 × 25%
	tax written down value	10,546			14,062 − 3,516
4	sale proceeds	(5,000)			
	balancing allowance	5,546	1,664	5	(10,546 − 5,000) × 25%

Do you understand?

1   An asset costing $40,000 is expected to last for three years, after which it can be sold for $16,000. The corporation tax rate is 30%, tax-allowable depreciation at 25% is available and the cost of capital is 10%. Tax is payable at the end of each financial year.

Capital expenditure occurs on the last day of a financial year and the tax-allowable depreciation is claimed as early as possible.

What is the cash flow in respect of the tax-allowable depreciation that will be used at time 2 of the net present value calculation?

A $1,688

B $2,250

C $5,624

D $7,500

1 A. t0 tax-allowable depreciation $10,000 ($40,000 × 25%), t1 tax-allowable depreciation $7,500 (($40,000 − $10,000) × 25%), t2 tax-allowable depreciation $5,625 (($40,000 - $10,000 - $7,500) × 25%), t2 tax saving $1,688 ($5,625 × 30%).

Incorporating working capital

The treatment of working capital is as follows:

initial investment is a cash outflow at the start of the project

if the investment is increased, the increase is a relevant cash outflow

if the investment is decreased, the decrease is a relevant cash inflow

working capital is 'released' at the end of the project, leading to a cash inflow.

Do you understand?

1 A new project is expected to generate sales of 55,000 units per year. The selling price is expected to be $3.50 per unit in the first year, growing at 6% per annum. The project is expected to last for three years. Working capital equal to 12% of annual sales is required and needs to be in place at the start of each year.

What is the cash flow in respect of working capital that will be used at time 2 of the net present value calculation?

A $(25,955)

B $(24,486)

C $(1,386)

D $(1,469)

1   D. Annual sales are $192,500 (55,000 × $3.50). t1 working capital $24,486 ($192,500 × 1.06 × 12%), t2 working capital $25,955 ($192,500 × 1.06² × 12%), increase in working capital for t2 $1,469 ($25,955 − $24,486).

1 Which of the following statements is correct?

    A   Tax allowable depreciation is a relevant cash flow when evaluating borrowing to buy compared to leasing as a financing choice

    B   Asset replacement decisions require relevant cash flows to be discounted by the after-tax cost of debt

    C   If capital is rationed, divisible investment projects can be ranked by the profitability index when determining the optimum investment schedule

    D   Government restrictions on bank lending are associated with soft capital rationing

2 A company has 31 December as its accounting year end. On 1 January 20X7 a new machine costing $2,000,000 is purchased. The company expects to sell the machine on 31 December 20X8 for $350,000.

The rate of corporation tax for the company is 30%. Tax-allowable depreciation is obtained at 25% on the reducing balance basis, and a balancing allowance is available on disposal of the asset. The company makes sufficient profits to obtain relief for tax-allowable depreciation as soon as they arise.

If the company's cost of capital is 15% per annum, what is the present value of the tax savings from the tax-allowable depreciation at 1 January 20X7 (to the nearest thousand dollars)?

    A $391,000

    B $248,000

    C $263,000

    D $719,000

3 A company has a 'money' cost of capital of 21% per annum. The inflation is currently estimated at 8% per annum.

What is the 'real' cost of capital (to the nearest whole number)?

4 Company H plans to purchase a machine costing $18,000 to save labour costs. Labour savings would be $9,000 in the first year and labour rates in the second year will increase by 10%. The estimated average annual rate of inflation is 8% and the company's real cost of capital is estimated at 12%. The machine has a two year life with an estimated actual salvage value of £5,000 receivable at the end of year 2. All cash flows occur at the year end.

What is the negative NPV (to the nearest $10) of the proposed investment?

    A $50

    B $270

    C $380

    D $650

5   A project has an initial outflow at time 0 when an asset is bought, then
a series of revenue inflows at the end of each year, and then finally
sales proceeds from the sale of the asset. Its NPV is £12,000 when
general inflation is zero % per year.

**If general inflation were to rise to 7% per year, and all revenue
inflows were subject to this rate of inflation but the initial
expenditure and resale value of the asset were not subject to
inflation, what would happen to the NPV?**

A   The NPV would remain the same

B   The NPV would rise

C   The NPV would fall

D   The NPV could rise or fall

5 **Investment and capital rationing**

The following topics are covered in this chapter:
- Asset investment decisions
- Capital rationing

5.1 ASSET INVESTMENT DECISIONS

LEARNING SUMMARY

After studying this section you should be able to:

- evaluate leasing and borrowing to buy using the before and after tax costs of debt
- evaluate asset replacement decisions using equivalent annual cost.

Lease versus buy

A separate decision to the investment decision is how to finance the asset purchase. The choice is between leasing or buying.

DEFINITION **Leasing** – effectively financing the purchase of the asset with the lease contract.

DEFINITION **Buying** – acquiring the asset with separate finance arranged for the purchase.

KEY POINT The net present values (NPVs) of the two financing options are calculated and the lowest cost option selected. The cash flows of this option would then be included as relevant cash flows in the NPV calculation for the project.

> Watch out for timing – if the lease payment is at the start of a year the tax saving will be two years later if tax is paid a year in arrears.

| Cash flows for leasing | - the lease payments (often paid at the start of a year)
- the tax relief on the lease payments |

| Cash flows for buying | - the purchase payment and scrap value
- the tax savings from tax-allowable depreciation |

use the post-tax cost of borrowing for both sets of calculations.

cost of borrowing × (1 – tax rate)

Replacement decisions

KEY POINT If a capital asset is to be replaced, there are different potential replacement strategies. Equivalent available assets may last for different lengths of time, assets may need to be replaced at regular intervals.

In order to make the different strategies comparable, use equivalent annual costs (EACs). The decision that has the lowest EAC will be the one chosen:

equivalent annual cost	assumptions:
$=$ **present value (PV) of costs** **annuity factor for year n** n = the length of the replacement period in years	trading cash flows from the use of the asset are ignored as they are assumed to be similar whichever asset/replacement cycle is chosen
	operating efficiencies of machines will be similar with differing machines and with differing ages
	the assets will be replaced into perpetuity or at least into the foreseeable future
	tax, inflation and non-financial aspects are ignored.

For example, a machine costs $15,000. Running costs in the first year are anticipated to be $3,000 and in the second year would be $3,600. If the machine were sold after one year the anticipated sales proceeds are $7,000. If used for another year and then sold the proceeds would fall to $4,000.

The optimal replacement cycle for the machine if the cost of capital is 11% is:

1 year cycle

t0 (15,000) × 1 = (15,000)

t1 [(3,000) + 7,000] × 0.901 = 3,604

Total PV of cycle = $(11,396)

EAC = (11,396)/0.901 = $(12,648)

2 year cycle

t0 (15,000) × 1 = (15,000)

t1 (3,000) × 0.901 = (2,703)

t2 [(3,600) + 4,000] × 0.812 = 325

Total PV of cycle = $(17,378)

EAC = (17,378)/1.713 = $(10,145)

= the 2 year cycle is the cheaper option.

Do you understand?

1   The present value of costs for a one year machine replacement is $(10,001) and a two year replacement $(18,350)

Using a cost of capital of 10%, what is the optimal replacement cycle?

A   One year

B   Two years

5.2 CAPITAL RATIONING

LEARNING SUMMARY

After studying this section you should be able to:

- evaluate investment decisions under single period capital rationing.

KEY POINT Shareholder wealth is maximised if a company undertakes all positive NPV projects it has available. Capital rationing is where there are insufficient funds to do this.

DEFINITION Hard capital rationing – an absolute limit on financing available is imposed by the funders of the business. The business cannot raise further cash.

DEFINITION Soft capital rationing – an internally imposed limit on investment capital. This is contrary to the rational view of shareholder wealth maximisation.

Divisible projects and the profitability index

KEY POINT If a project is divisible then any proportion of the project may be undertaken and the returns from the project are expected to be generated in exact proportion to the amount of investment undertaken.

The profitability index (PI) can be used to rank projects against each other in order to determine which ones to undertake to maximise the total NPV earned from the available capital.

profitability index

=

net present value
initial investment

Indivisible projects

KEY POINT If a project is indivisible then it must be done in its entirety or not at all. When projects are indivisible the optimal combination of projects to undertake with the capital available can only be found by trial and error.

Mutually exclusive projects

KEY POINT When certain projects cannot be done together, perhaps because they are different uses of the same asset, each combination of investments should be tried to determine which gives the highest overall NPV.

Do you understand?

1 A company has a number of projects available but has a limit of $20,000 on its capital investment funds. Each project has an initial outlay followed by a constant annual cash flow in perpetuity, commencing in one year's time. The projects are as follows:

Project	Initial outlay ($)	Inflow per year ($)
E	6,000	900
F	8,000	1,000
G	10,000	3,500
H	12,000	3,600
I	20,000	4,600

The company's cost of capital is 10% per year and all projects are independent and indivisible.

What is the maximum net present value that can be generated?

A $26,000

B $27,000

C $28,000

D $45,000

1   Four projects, A, B, C and D, are available to a company which is facing shortages of capital over the next year but expects capital to be freely available thereafter.

	A	B	C	D
	$000	$000	$000	$000
Total capital required over life of project	20	30	40	50
Capital required in next year	20	10	30	40
Net present value of project at company's cost of capital	60	40	80	80

In what sequence should the projects be selected if the company wishes to maximise net present values?

A   A, C, D, B

B   B, A, C, D

C   B, C, A, D

D   C, D, A, B

2   Company F buys a machine for $10,000 and sells it for $2,000 at time 3. Running costs of the machine are: time 1 = $3,000; time 2 = $5,000; time 3 = $7,000.

If a series of machines are bought, run and sold on an infinite cycle of replacements, what is the equivalent annual cost of the machine if the discount rate is 10%?

A $22,114

B $8,892

C $8,288

D $7,371

3   Company J has four independent projects available:

	Capital needed at time 0	NPV
	$	$
Project 5	10,000	30,000
Project 6	8,000	25,000
Project 7	12,000	30,000
Project 8	16,000	36,000

If the company has $32,000 to invest at time 0, and each project is infinitely divisible, but none can be delayed, what is the maximum NPV that can be earned?

A $85,000

B $89,500

C $102,250

D $103,000

4 **In relation to a long-term lease, which of the following statements is NOT correct?**

A   All the risks and rewards of ownership transfer to the lessee

B   The asset and lease obligation will be recorded in the statement of financial position

C   The lease period will cover almost all of the leased asset's useful economic life

D   The lessor will be responsible for repairs and maintenance of the leased asset

6 Investment appraisal - uncertainty

The following topics are covered in this chapter:
- Risk versus uncertainty
- Investment appraisal techniques under uncertainty

6.1 RISK VERSUS UNCERTAINTY

LEARNING SUMMARY

After studying this section you should be able to:

- describe and discuss the difference between risk and uncertainty in relation to probabilities and increasing project life.

KEY POINT Risk and uncertainty affect investment appraisals because the appraisals are an attempt to forecast the future of such things as cash flows, inflation rates, taxation laws, cost of capital, etc., none of which may be known for certain over the life of the investment.

Risk - quantifiable ········▸ possible outcomes have associated probabilities, therefore allow the use of mathematical techniques:

- expected values

- simulation

- adjusted payback

- risk-adjusted discount rates

Uncertainty - unquantifiable ········▸ outcomes cannot be mathematically modelled, therefore:

- set minimum payback periods

- make prudent estimates of cash flows in the appraisal

- assess best and worst case scenarios

- use sensitivity analysis

In investment appraisal, the areas of concern are therefore the accuracy of the estimates concerning:

project cash flow

predicted cash flows and associated probabilities

discount rate used.

6.2 INVESTMENT APPRAISAL TECHNIQUES UNDER UNCERTAINTY

LEARNING SUMMARY

After studying this section you should be able to:

- apply sensitivity analysis to investment projects and discuss the usefulness of it in assisting investment decisions

- apply probability analysis to investment projects and discuss the usefulness of it in assisting investment decisions

- apply and discuss other techniques of adjusting for risk and uncertainty in investment appraisal.

Sensitivity analysis

KEY POINT Sensitivity analysis takes each uncertain factor in turn, and calculates the change that would be necessary in that factor before the original decision is reversed, it involves posing 'what-if' questions.

Calculating sensitivity – the sensitivity margin

$$= \frac{\text{Net present value (NPV)}}{\begin{array}{c}\text{Present value (PV) of cash flows}\\\text{under consideration}\end{array}} \times 100$$

for example, the NPV of a project is $28,400, the PV of the initial investment is $220,000 and the PV of the sales revenue is $828,000

- the sensitivity to the initial investment is 12.9% ($28,400/$220,000 × 100)

- the sensitivity to the selling price is 3.4% ($28,400/$828,000 × 100)

the lower the sensitivity of an input variable, the more sensitive the project NPV is to changes in that input variable.

Advantages of sensitivity analysis	Disadvantages of sensitivity analysis
simple to calculate and evaluate	assumes variables change independently of each other
provides further information to allow management to make subjective judgements	only assesses the impact of one variable changing at a time
identifies critical estimates	does not assess the likelihood of a variable changing
	does not directly identify a correct accept or reject decision for a project

Probability analysis

When there are several possible outcomes for a decision and probabilities can be assigned to each, a probability distribution of expected cash flows can be estimated, recognising that there are several possible outcomes, not just one. This could then be used to:

calculate an expected value

measure risk by:

calculating the worst possible outcome and its probability

calculating the probability that the project will fail

assessing the standard deviation of the outcomes

> **KEY POINT** An expected value is a weighted average of all possible outcomes, it calculates the average return that will be made if a decision is repeated again and again.

Expected value (EV) =	Σpx	(x = value of each possible outcome)
		(p = probability)

Do you understand?

1   A company has to choose between three mutually exclusive projects, the outcomes of which depend on the state of the economy. The following estimates have been made:

State of the economy	poor	good	excellent
Probability	0.4	0.5	0.1
Project:	NPV ($000)	NPV ($000)	NPV ($000)
A	150	70	10
B	(10)	40	600
C	75	75	125

Which project should be selected on the basis of expected NPVs?

A

B

C

---

1   A.

EV project A = 150 × 0.4 + 70 × 0.5 + 10 × 0.1 = 96
EV project B = (10) × 0.4 + 40 × 0.5 + 600 × 0.1 = 76
EV project C = 75 × 0.4 + 75 × 0.5 + 125 × 0.1 = 80

Advantages of expected values	Disadvantages of expected values
deals with multiple outcomes	subjective probabilities
quantifies probabilities	answer is only a long-run average
relatively simple calculation	ignores variability of payoffs
assists decision making	risk neutral decision, i.e. ignores investors' attitudes to risk

Expected values are appropriate to use when:

- there is a reasonable basis for making the forecasts and estimating the probabilities of different outcomes

- the decision is relatively small in relation to the business, so the risk is small in magnitude

- it is for a category of decisions that are often made.

Other techniques

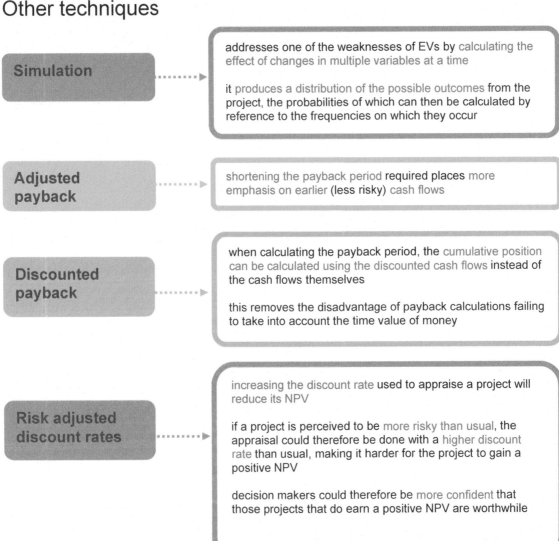

Simulation

addresses one of the weaknesses of EVs by calculating the effect of changes in multiple variables at a time

it produces a distribution of the possible outcomes from the project, the probabilities of which can then be calculated by reference to the frequencies on which they occur

Adjusted payback

shortening the payback period required places more emphasis on earlier (less risky) cash flows

Discounted payback

when calculating the payback period, the cumulative position can be calculated using the discounted cash flows instead of the cash flows themselves

this removes the disadvantage of payback calculations failing to take into account the time value of money

Risk adjusted discount rates

increasing the discount rate used to appraise a project will reduce its NPV

if a project is perceived to be more risky than usual, the appraisal could therefore be done with a higher discount rate than usual, making it harder for the project to gain a positive NPV

decision makers could therefore be more confident that those projects that do earn a positive NPV are worthwhile

Do you understand?

1. Company F is currently evaluating a project which requires investments of $12,000 now, and $4,800 at the end of year 1. The cash inflow from the project will be $16,800 at the end of year 2 and $14,400 at the end of year 3. The cost of capital is 15%.

   What is the discounted payback period (DPP) and the net present value (NPV)?

   A   DPP 2.00 years, NPV $6,000

   B   DPP 2.36 years, NPV $4,440

   C   DPP 2.00 years, NPV $4,440

   D   DPP 2.36 years, NPV $6,000

---

1 D.

Year	Cash flow ($)	Discount factor (15%)	Present value ($)	Cumulative present value ($)
0	(12,000)	1.000	(12,000)	(12,000)
1	(4,800)	0.870	(4,176)	(16,176)
2	16,800	0.756	12,701	(3,475)
3	14,400	0.658	9,475	6,000
NPV			6,000	

Discounted payback period 2.36 years (2 + (3,475/(3,475 + 6,000))).

Company J plans to buy a new machine. The cost of the machine, payable immediately, is $800,000 and the machine has an expected life of five years. Additional investment in working capital of $90,000 will be required at the start of the first year of operation. At the end of five years, the machine will be sold for scrap, with the scrap value expected to be 5% of the initial purchase cost of the machine. The machine will not be replaced.

Production and sales from the new machine are expected to be 100,000 units per year. Each unit can be sold for $16 per unit and will incur variable costs of $11 per unit. Incremental fixed costs arising from the operation of the machine will be $160,000 per year.

Company J has an after-tax cost of capital of 11% which it uses as a discount rate in investment appraisal. The company pays profit tax one year in arrears at an annual rate of 30% per year. Tax allowable depreciation and inflation should be ignored.

1   Calculate the net present value of investing in the new machine and advise whether the investment is financially acceptable.

2   Calculate the internal rate of return of investing in the new machine and advise whether the investment is financially acceptable.

3   Explain briefly the meaning of the term 'sensitivity analysis' in the context of investment appraisal.

4   Calculate the sensitivity of the investment in the new machine to a change in selling price and to a change in discount rate, and comment on your findings.

7.1 THE NATURE AND ELEMENTS OF WORKING CAPITAL

LEARNING SUMMARY

After studying this section you should be able to:

- describe the nature of working capital and identify its elements

- identify the objectives of working capital management in terms of liquidity and profitability, and discuss the conflict between them

- discuss the central role of working capital management in financial management.

The elements of working capital

KEY POINT Working capital is the capital available for conducting the day-to-day operations of an organisation; normally the excess of current assets over current liabilities.

Working capital management is the management of all aspects of both current assets and current liabilities, to minimise the risk of insolvency while maximising the return on assets.

Current assets **require funding**	········▶	consider reducing funding levels for example: - cash required to buy inventory - cash delayed by offering credit to customers
Current liabilities **provide funding**	········▶	consider increasing funding levels for example: - cash delayed by accepting credit from suppliers

Investing in working capital has a cost:

- the cost of funding it, or

- the opportunity cost of lost investments because cash is tied up in working capital and unavailable for other uses.

The objectives of working capital management

KEY POINT The main objective of working capital management is to get the balance of current assets and current liabilities right.

Working capital management is a trade-off between profitability and liquidity:

| Liquidity

ensuring current assets are sufficiently liquid to minimise the risk of insolvency |

> if a business has large amounts of cash then it should be able to pay its bills on time – liquidity is the priority

| Profitability

investing in less liquid assets in order to maximise return |

> if cash could have been invested elsewhere, for example in offering better credit terms to customers to attract more business, this would potentially increase profitability but at the expense of liquidity

The role of working capital management

KEY POINT A business which chooses to have a **lower** level of working capital is said to have an **aggressive approach – higher profitability and higher risk.**

KEY POINT A business which chooses to have a **higher** level of working capital is said to have a **conservative approach – lower profitability and lower risk.**

| Over capitalisation |

- excessive current assets and low current liabilities mean that the business is over-capitalised
- there has been an over investment by the business in current assets.
- profitability will suffer as a result

| Overtrading |

if a business does not have access to sufficient capital to fund increases in profitability and investment in non-current assets and working capital, it is said to be "over trading"

this can cause serious trouble for the business if it is unable to pay its commitments, indicators are:
- a rapid increase in revenue
- a rapid increase in the volume of current assets
- most of the increase in assets being financed by credit
- a dramatic drop in the liquidity ratios

7.2 WORKING CAPITAL RATIOS

LEARNING SUMMARY

After studying this section you should be able to:

- explain and apply relevant accounting ratios

- explain the cash operating cycle

- calculate the level of working capital investment in current assets and discuss the key factors to determine the level required.

Liquidity ratios

Current ratio measures how much of the total current assets are financed by current liabilities	= $\dfrac{\text{Current assets}}{\text{Current liabilities}}$ a measure of 2:1 means that current liabilities can be paid twice over out of existing current assets
Quick ratio measures how well current liabilities are covered by liquid assets it is particularly useful where inventory holding periods are long	= $\dfrac{\text{Current assets - inventory}}{\text{Current liabilities}}$ a measure of 1:1 means that the entity is able to meet existing liabilities if they all fall due at once

Cash operating cycle

KEY POINT The cash operating cycle (working capital cycle) is the length of time between the company's outlay on raw materials, wages and other expenditures and the inflow of cash from the sale of goods.

The faster a firm can 'push' items around the cycle, the lower the total working capital and the lower its investment in working capital needs to be:

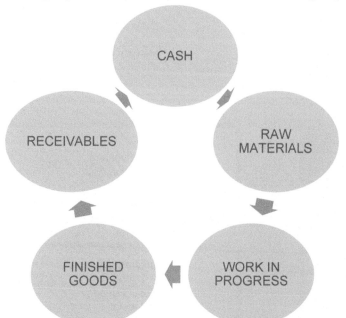

Raw materials holding period	X
Less: payables payment period	(X)
WIP holding period	X
Finished goods holding period	X
Receivables collection period	X
Cash operating cycle	X

Factors affecting the length of the cycle depend on:	
liquidity versus profitability decisions	management efficiency
terms of trade	industry norms

KEY POINT The optimum level of working capital is the amount that results in no idle cash or unused inventory but that does not put a strain on liquid resources.

Do you understand?

1   Which of the following will shorten the cash operating cycle?

    A   An increase in the raw materials inventory holding period

    B   An increase in the trade payable days

    C   An increase in the trade receivables days

    D   An increase in the production period

1 B.

Cash operating cycle ratios

Inventory holding period
the length of time inventory is held between purchase or completion and sale

$$= \frac{\text{Inventory}}{\text{Cost of sales}} \times 365$$

Raw material inventory holding period
the length of time raw materials are held between purchase and being used in production

$$= \frac{\text{Raw material inventory}}{\text{Material usage}} \times 365$$

Work in progress (WIP) holding period
the length of time goods spend in production

$$= \frac{\text{WIP inventory}}{\text{Production cost}} \times 365$$

Finished goods inventory holding period
the length of time finished goods are held between completion of purchase and sale

$$= \frac{\text{Finished goods inventory}}{\text{Cost of goods sold}} \times 365$$

Trade receivables days
the length of time credit is extended to customers

$$= \frac{\text{Trade receivables}}{\text{Credit sales}} \times 365$$

Trade payables days
the average period of credit extended by suppliers

$$= \frac{\text{Trade payables}}{\text{Credit purchases}} \times 365$$

Working capital turnover
measures how efficiently management is utilising its investment in working capital to generate sales

$$= \frac{\text{Sales revenue}}{\text{Net working capital}}$$

If the exact figure is not given, use the closest approximation.

Do you understand?

1   Company C makes place mats. The company buys raw materials from suppliers that allow the company 2.5 months credit. The raw materials remain in inventory for 2 months and it takes Company C 2 months to produce the goods, which are sold immediately production is completed. Customers take an average of 1.5 months to pay.

What is Company C's cash operating cycle?

A   2 months

B   2.5 months

C   3 months

D   7 months

1   C. 2 − 2.5 + 2 + 1.5 = 3 months.

1 **Select whether the following statements are True or False:**

	True	False
Working capital should increase as sales increase		
An increase in the cash operating cycle will decrease profitability		
Overtrading is also known as under-capitalisation		

2 **Which of the following might be associated with a shortening working capital cycle?**

    A   Lower net operating cash flow

    B   Increasing tax-allowable depreciation expenditure

    C   Slower inventory turnover

    D   Taking longer to pay suppliers

3 The following information has been calculated for Company F:

Trade receivables collection period	10 weeks
Raw material inventory turnover period	6 weeks
Work in progress inventory turnover period	2 weeks
Trade payables payment period	7 weeks
Finished goods inventory turnover period	6 weeks

What is the length of the cash operating cycle?

4 A company sells inventory for cash to a customer, at a selling price which is below the cost of the inventory items.

How will this transaction affect the current ratio and the quick ratio immediately after the transaction?

Ratio	Increase	Decrease
Current ratio		
Quick ratio		

8.1 WORKING CAPITAL MANAGEMENT – INVENTORY CONTROL

LEARNING SUMMARY

After studying this section you should be able to:

- discuss, apply and evaluate the use of relevant techniques in managing inventory, including the economic order quantity model and just in time techniques.

The objectives of inventory control

KEY POINT Inventory is a major investment for many companies. Manufacturing companies can easily carry inventory equivalent to between 50% and 100% of the revenue of the business. It is therefore essential to reduce the levels of inventory held to the necessary minimum.

Liquidity	reducing inventory to the lowest possible amount to minimise the level of funding needed
Profitability	ensuring that sufficient inventory is held so that it does not run out and disrupt business

The problems associated with inventory control are:

Inventory levels too high	keeping inventory levels high is expensive owing to: • the foregone interest that is lost (or borrowing interest that is paid) from tying up capital in inventory • holding costs: storage stores administration risk of theft, damage or obsolescence
Inventory levels too low	if inventory levels are kept too low, the business faces alternative problems: • high re-order costs and/or set up costs • stock outs: lost contribution production stoppages emergency orders • lost quantity discounts

The objective of good inventory management is therefore to determine the optimum re-order level and the optimum re-order quantity.

This means striking a balance between holding costs on one hand and stock out and re-order costs on the other.

> **DEFINITION   Re-order level** – how many items should be left in inventory when the next order is placed.

> **DEFINITION   Re-order quantity** – how many items should be ordered when the order is placed.

Economic order quantity(EOQ)

KEY POINT For businesses that do not use just in time (JIT) inventory management systems there is an optimum order quantity for inventory orders, the EOQ. The aim of the EOQ model is to minimise the total cost of holding and ordering inventory.

The EOQ formula is given in the exam.

Economic order quantity

$$= \sqrt{\left(\frac{2CoD}{Ch}\right)}$$

Co = cost per order
D = annual demand
Ch = cost of holding one unit for one year

for example,
annual demand for a product is 100,000 units
the purchase price is \$10 per unit and the company's cost of finance is 20% per annum
other holding costs of inventory total \$0.50 per unit per month
ordering costs are \$125 each time an order is made

D = 100,000 per annum

Co = \$125

Ch = (\$0.50 × 12) + (\$10 × 20%)
   = \$8 per unit per annum

EOQ = √(2 × \$125 × 100,000/\$8)
    = 1,768 units per order.

Do you understand?

1   Company G is a retailer of sweet boxes. The company has an annual demand of 120,000 units. The costs incurred each time an order is placed are \$200. The carrying costs per unit of the item each month is estimated at \$3. The purchase price of each unit is \$4.

When using the economic order quantity formula to find the optimal quantity to be ordered, which of the following amounts are NOT included in the calculation?

A   Cost per order (\$200)

B   Carrying cost per order (\$3)

C   Purchase price per unit (\$4)

D   Estimated usage (120,000 units per annum)

1. C

Other formulae are:

Annual holding costs = Ch × EOQ/2

Annual ordering costs = Co × D/EOQ

Economic order quantity with quantity discounts

KEY POINT Discounts may be offered for ordering in large quantities.

If the EOQ is smaller than the order size needed for a discount, should the order size be increased above the EOQ?

To work out the answer you should carry out the following steps:

Step 1	calculate EOQ, ignoring discounts
Step 2	if the EOQ is below the quantity qualifying for a discount, calculate the total annual inventory cost arising from using the EOQ
Step 3	recalculate total annual inventory costs using the order size required to just obtain each discount
Step 4	compare the cost of Steps 2 and 3 with the saving from the discount, and select the minimum cost alternative
Step 5	repeat for all discount levels (if required)

For example, a company has annual demand for its product of 50,000 units. Each unit costs $1.50. Ordering costs are $55 per order and the annual holding cost per unit is $1.

Determine if the optimum ordering quantity would change if the supplier offered a discount of 1% as long as at least 4,000 units were ordered each time:

Step 1	EOQ = √(2 × $55 × 50,000/$1) = 2,345 units per order
Step 2	total costs at 2,345 units (purchasing + ordering + holding costs): (50,000 × $1.50) + (50,000/2,345 × $55) + (2,345/2 × $1) = $75,000 + $1,173 + $1,173 = $77,346
Step 3	total costs at 4,000 units: (50,000 × $1.50 × 99%) + (50,000/4,000 × $55) + (4,000/2 × $1) = $74,250 + $688 + $2,000 = $76,938
Step 4	saving = $408 ($77,346 - $76,938), therefore the optimum ordering quantity rises to 4,000 units.

Re-order level (ROL)

KEY POINT Having decided how much inventory to reorder, the next problem is when to reorder. The firm needs to identify a level of inventory which can be reached before an order needs to be placed.

re-order level with with **known demand** and lead time	┈┈▶	when demand and lead time are known with certainty the ROL may be calculated exactly **ROL = demand in the lead time**	
re-order level with with **variable demand** or lead time	┈┈▶	when there is uncertainty over demand or lead time then an optimum level of buffer inventory must be found, which will depend on such things as the variability of demand, the cost of holding inventory and the cost of stock outs	The calculation for the re-order level with variable demand or lead time is not required for the exam.

Do you understand?

1   Which of the following statements are true:

(1)   The re-order level is the measure of inventory at which a replenishment order should be made

(2)   Use of a re-order level build in a measure of safety inventory and minimises the risk of the organisation running out of inventory.

A   (1) and (2)

B   (1)

C   (2)

D   neither

1. A.

Inventory management systems

Bin systems	when inventory reaches a pre-set minimum level in a bin, it is re-ordered
Periodic review systems	inventory levels are reviewed at fixed intervals and then topped up to a pre-determined level
Just in time (JIT) systems	JIT is a series of manufacturing and supply chain techniques that aim to minimise inventory levels and improve customer service by manufacturing not only at the exact time customers require, but also in the exact quantities they need and at competitive prices
	in JIT systems, the balancing act is dispensed with, inventory is reduced to an absolute minimum or eliminated altogether

1   **Which of the following is an aim of a Just in Time system of inventory control?**

    A   Increase in capital tied up in inventory

    B   Creation of an inflexible production process

    C   Elimination of all activities performed that do not add value

    D   Lowering of inventory ordering costs

9.1 WORKING CAPITAL MANAGEMENT – ACCOUNTS RECEIVABLE

LEARNING SUMMARY

After studying this section you should be able to:

- discuss, apply and evaluate the use of relevant techniques in managing accounts receivable.

The objectives of a credit policy

KEY POINT Management must establish a credit policy. The optimum level of trade credit extended represents a balance between two factors, liquidity and profitability. This trade-off is a key factor in determining the organisation's working capital investment.

| Liquidity | ┈┈┈▶ | collecting sales receipts as quickly as possible to reduce the cost of financing the receivables balance |

| Profitability | ┈┈┈▶ | extending the credit period to customers to encourage additional sales |

An organisation's credit policy will be influenced by:

demand for products	financing costs
competitors' terms	costs of credit control
risk of irrecoverable debts	

A credit policy has four key aspects:

1. Assess creditworthiness	new customers immediately
	existing customers periodically
2. Credit limits	amount of credit
	length of time allowed before payment
3. Invoice promptly and collect overdue debts	to reduce risk of default
4. Monitor the credit system	aged receivable reports
	ratios
	statistical data

Accounts receivable calculations

- credit is offered to customers to encourage sales

- prompt payment discounts are offered to customers to encourage faster payment

Cost of financing receivables

finance cost = receivables balance x interest rate

for example,
company D has sales of $50m for the previous year receivables days are 57 and receivables are financed using an overdraft costing 6% per annum

receivables balance = 57 × $50m/365 = $7,808,219

finance cost = $7,808,219 × 6% = $468,493

Cost of offering early settlement discounts

annual cost of discount =
$(1 + (discount/amount\ left\ to\ pay))^{no.\ of\ periods} - 1$

no. of periods =   365 or 52 or 12

———————————————

no. of days or weeks or months earlier the money is received

for example,
a company is offering a 2% discount to receivables if they agree to pay within 30 days, the current receivables days figure is 65, receivables are financed using an overdraft costing 20%

effective annual cost = $[1 + 2/98]^{(365/35)} - 1 = 0.23452$ or 23.5%

if the company offers the discount, it will save interest at a rate of 20% on its overdraft but the discount will cost 23.5%, so the discount should not be offered

Do you understand?

1   Mike Co usually takes 2 months to collect its debts from credit customers. It has just issued an invoice to Bryan Co for $100 and offers a cash discount of 2% if payment is made within 1 month.

What is the effective annualised cost of the discount if Bryan Co does settle within 1 month?

A   27.4%

B   34.4%

C   20.0%

D   32.6%

Invoice discounting and factoring

> **KEY POINT** Invoice discounting and factoring are both ways of speeding up the receipt of funds from accounts receivable and therefore of reducing the funding need but they both come with costs attached.

Invoice discounting is a method of raising finance against the security of receivables, up to 80% of the debt value is advanced, however there is a finance cost:

Advantages	Disadvantages
short term cash boost	expensive in the long term
customer is unaware	extra administration costs

Invoice factoring is outsourcing of the credit control department to a third party for a charge, factoring may also be on a without recourse basis (factor pays even if the customer doesn't):

Advantages	Disadvantages
short term cash boost	expensive in the long term
administration savings	customer is aware and may not like it

Managing foreign trade

> **KEY POINT** Overseas accounts receivable bring additional risks that need to be managed.
>
> **Export credit risk** is the risk of failure or delay in collecting payments due from foreign customers.
>
> **Foreign exchange risk** is the risk that the value of the currency will change between the date of the contract and the date of settlement.
>
> Note that the same risks apply to trade payables.

9.2 WORKING CAPITAL MANAGEMENT – ACCOUNTS PAYABLE

LEARNING SUMMARY

After studying this section you should be able to:

- discuss, apply and evaluate the use of relevant techniques in managing accounts payable.

The objectives of obtaining trade credit

> **KEY POINT** Trade credit is the simplest and most important source of short-term finance for many entities. Again, it is a balancing act between profitability and liquidity.

Liquidity	┈┈┈▶	delaying payments to suppliers to obtain a 'free' source of finance
Profitability	┈┈┈▶	delaying too long may cause difficulties for the company in the long term

By delaying payment to suppliers, organisations face possible problems:

supplier may refuse to supply in the future	there may be a loss of reputation
supplier may only supply on a cash basis	supplier may increase prices in the future

Do you understand?

1   In order to improve operational cash flows, indicate whether a company would need to increase or decrease their receivables balance and payables balance.

    A   Increase receivables and increase payables

    B   Increase receivables and decrease payables

    C   Decrease receivables and decrease payables

    D   Decrease receivables and increase payables

1 D.

1 Bramwell has an accounts receivables turnover of 10.5 times, an inventory turnover of 4 times and payables turnover of 8 times.

What is Bramwell's cash operating cycle (assume 365 days in a year)?

A   80.38 days

B   6.50 days

C   22.50 days

D   171.64 days

2 **Which THREE of the following would be key aspects of a company's accounts receivable credit policy?**

A   Assessing creditworthiness

B   Checking credit limits

C   Invoicing promptly and collecting overdue debts

D   Delaying payments to obtain a 'free' source of finance

3 Generally, increasing payables days suggests advantage is being taken of available credit but there are risks involved.

Which of the following is unlikely to be one of the risks involved in increasing payables days?

A   Customer bargaining power increasing

B   Losing supplier goodwill

C   Losing prompt payment discounts

D   Suppliers increasing the price to compensate

10 Cash and funding strategies

The following topics are covered in this chapter:
- Holding and managing cash
- Strategies for funding working capital

10.1 HOLDING AND MANAGING CASH

LEARNING SUMMARY

After studying this section you should be able to:

- explain the various reasons for holding cash and discuss and apply the use of relevant techniques in managing cash.

The reasons for holding cash

The optimum level of cash represents a balance between two factors, liquidity and profitability:

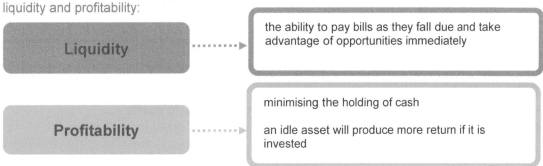

| Liquidity | ┄┄┄► | the ability to pay bills as they fall due and take advantage of opportunities immediately |

| Profitability | ┄┄┄► | minimising the holding of cash

an idle asset will produce more return if it is invested |

An organisation will have the following motives for holding cash:

transactions motive	to meet day-to-day expenses
precautionary motive	to meet unplanned expenditure
investment motive	to take advantage of investment opportunities

Failure to hold enough cash can lead to:

loss of settlement discounts	not enough cash available to pay suppliers early
loss of supplier goodwill	too many delayed payments can lead to issues
poor industrial relations	from delay in workers being paid
potential liquidation	if creditors bring company into administration for non-payment

Cash budgets and cash flow forecasts

DEFINITION Cash budgets – a plan for cash receipts and payments for a future period, after taking any action necessary to bring the forecast into line with the overall business plan.

Cash budgets are used to:

- assess and integrate operating budgets
- plan for cash shortages and surpluses
- compare with actual spending.

Cash flow forecasts can be prepared based on:

- a receipts and payments forecast

- a statement of financial position forecast

- working capital ratios.

Do you understand?

1   Which of the following should not be included in a cash flow forecast?

    A   Funds from the issue of share capital

    B   Repayment of a bank loan

    C   Receipts of dividends from outside a business

    D   Revaluation of a non-current asset

1. D.

When answering exam questions on the preparation of cash flow forecasts use a step approach:

Step 1 – prepare a proforma

Month	1	2	3	
	$	$	$	
Receipts	x	x	x	use a separate line for each type of receipt
Sub total	x	x	x	the total of all receipts
Payments	x	x	x	use a separate line for each type of payment
Sub total	x	x	x	the total of all payments
Net cash flow	x	x	x	the difference between receipts and payments
Opening balance	x*	x**	x	*the balance at the start of the first month ** the closing balance from month one
Closing balance	x	x	x	opening balance +/- net cash flow for the month

Step 2 – fill in the simple figures

for example:

- wages and salaries

- fixed overhead expenses

- dividend payments

- purchase of non-current assets

Step 3 – work out the more complex figures

for example:

- sales receipts and purchases payments – from timings of credit periods

- purchases – based on production

- variable overheads – based on levels of production

An example of an extract from a cash flow forecast is:

Material usage quantities for a company are predicted to be as follows:

Month 1   2   3   4   5

(000) 10   12   14   16   18

Production costs are $5 per unit and suppliers are paid in the month after purchase. The company intends to increase stocks of materials by 2,000 units each month by the end of months 1 and 2 and by 1,000 units each month by the end of months 3, 4 and 5.

The cash payments for material purchases for months 3 to 5 are:

Month	3	4	5
Month of purchase	2	3	4
Purchase quantities (units)	12,000 + 2,000 = 14,000	14,000 + 1,000 = 15,000	16,000 + 1,000 = 17,000
Cash payments ($5 per unit)	$70,000	$75,000	$85,000

Do you understand?

1   Company R's projected revenue for 20X8 is $350,000. It is forecast that 12% of sales will occur in January and remaining sales will be equally spread amongst the other eleven months. All sales are on credit. Receivables accounts are settled 50% in the month of sale, 45% in the following month, and 5% are written off as bad debts after two months.

Which of the following amounts represent the budgeted cash collections for March?

A   £24,500

B   £26,600

C   £28,000

D   £32,900

1   B. Sales for January = $42,000 ($350,000 × 12%), for the other months $28,000 (($350,000 − $42,000)/11). Cash receipts in March = $26,600 (($28,000 × 50%) + ($28,000 × 45%)).

Cash management models

The Baumol cash management model

The EOQ formula is given in the exam.

Baumol cash management formula

$$Q = \sqrt{\left(\frac{2CoD}{Ch}\right)}$$

Co = the **brokerage cost** of making a securities trade or borrowing

D = **demand for cash** over the period

Ch = **opportunity cost of holding cash** (equals the rate of return generated by marketable securities or the cost of borrowing in order to hold cash)

for example,
a profitable company has a cash balance that is growing over time,
each month it generates $25,000 excess cash,
it intends to transfer this cash into a short-term deposit account which would earn 3% per annum,
every time it transfers money into the account it incurs a transaction fee of $25

the optimum amount of cash to be transferred each time is:

D = $25,000 × 12 = $300,000

Co = $25

Ch = $0.03

Q = √(2 × $25 × $300,000/$0.03) = $22,361

the optimum transaction value balances the transaction costs against the opportunity costs of holding cash:

transaction costs = D/Q × Co
= $300,000/$22,361 × $25 = $335

opportunity costs of holding cash = Q/2 × Ch
= $22.361/2 × $0.03 = $335

The Miller-Orr cash management model

The Miller-Orr formula is given in the exam.

KEY POINT The Miller-Orr model controls irregular movements of cash by the setting of upper and lower control limits on cash balances. It has the advantage of incorporating uncertainty in the cash outflows and inflows.

The Miller-Orr cash management formula

$$\text{Spread} = 3 \left(\frac{\frac{3}{4} \times \text{transaction cost} \times \text{variance of cash flows}}{\text{interest rate}} \right)^{1/3}$$

(1) Lower limit – must be given by the question.
(2) Upper limit = lower limit + spread.
(3) Return point = lower limit +1/3 × spread.

for example,
the cash balance at Company D fluctuates over time with some months seeing a large positive cash balance and others showing an overdraft.
The company wishes to control its cash more efficiently and take advantage of available short-term investments when it has surplus cash.
It wishes to maintain a minimum cash balance of $10,000.
The short-term investments earn interest at 0.04% per day.
If the transaction cost of switching cash between the current account and the company's short-term investments is $15 and the variance of the company's cash flows is $6 million per day, the spread, the return point and the upper limit, using the Miller-Orr model are:

spread = 3 × [0.75 × $15 × $6,000,000/0.0004]1/3 = $16,578

return point = $10,000 + ($^{1/3}$ × $16,578) = $15,526

upper limit = $10,000 + $16,578 = $26,578

Short-term investment and borrowing solutions

short-term cash investments - used for temporary cash surpluses

to weigh up an investment a company has to look at three potentially conflicting objectives and the factors surrounding them:
- liquidity – the cash must be available for use when needed as the surplus is only short-term
- safety – no risk of loss must be taken as once the surplus period is over the investment must be converted back into enough cash to meet the business needs
- profitability – subject to the above, the aim is to earn the highest possible after-tax returns

short-term borrowing

there are two main sources of bank lending:
- bank overdraft – flexible and cheap as only used when needed, but repayable on demand, may require security and interest rates can change
- bank loans – less flexible and more expensive as paying for a fixed period even if cash balances recover, but more secure

10.2 STRATEGIES FOR FUNDING WORKING CAPITAL

LEARNING SUMMARY

After studying this section you should be able to:

• describe and discuss the key factors in determining working capital funding strategies.

KEY POINT In the same way as for long-term investments, a firm must make a decision about what source of finance is best used for the funding of working capital requirements.

current assets are made up of two elements: ┈┈▶

permanent – the proportion of current assets that are effectively 'fixed', e.g. buffer inventory levels, minimum receivables and minimum cash balances

fluctuating – the proportion of current assets that changes, e.g. inventory above the buffer level, receivables above the minimum level

the **choice of funding working capital** is either from: ┈┈▶

short-term sources – cheaper due to lower risk for investor, but more risky as may not be renewed

long-term sources – more expensive than short-term but less risky

the **strategy** adopted **depends on management's attitude to risk** ┈┈▶

aggressive – finance most current assets, including permanent ones, with short-term finance. Risky but cheaper (more profitable)

conservative – finance most current assets, including a portion of fluctuating ones, with long-term finance. Safer but more expensive

matching – fluctuating current assets financed with short-term sources, permanent current assets financed by long-term sources

Do you understand?

1   Which of the following statements is/are true?

Statement 1 – an aggressive working capital investment policy aims to finance most of its current assets with long-term finance

Statement 2 – a conservative working capital investment policy aims to finance most of its current assets with short-term finance

A   1 and 2

B   1

C   2

D   Neither

Greene Co is a decentralised organisation whose different divisions have approached the matter of cash control in different ways, partly because of their different circumstances. Assume 365 days in a year.

The Northern division is facing a two-year major capital investment programme for which significant funds need to be raised to meet the steady demand for cash. The division intends to use the 'Baumol model' to decide when to raise funds, which will be done by selling off investments currently earning 5% per annum. The transaction cost of these sales will be $500 per transaction and the total amount needed over the two years is $2,000,000.

The Western division has no significant investment plans but finds itself regularly having to either sell investments to make funds available or invest surplus cash. This is because of the considerable variation in daily cash inflows which has been quantified as having a standard deviation of $7,000. As a result, the division uses the 'Miller-Orr model' to determine when to invest and when to make sales, using the same transaction cost and investment rate as the Northern division.

The Southern division has just been created to manufacture a product used by other divisions but mainly sold to outside customers. The coming month, Month 1, will be spent converting and equipping existing corporate premises at a total cash cost of $800,000. Production will start in Month 2 and sales in Month 3. Planned sales volumes are as follows.

Month	3	4	5	6	7
Sales volume (000s)	10	11	13	16	20

The product will sell for $24 per unit. 20% of sales will be for cash. Of the credit sales, 25% of credit customers (including other divisions) pay in the month following the sale, 50% will pay one month later and 25% after another month.

1   **How much finance should the Northern division raise in a single tranche according to the Baumol model?**

   A $14,142

   B $20,000

   C $141,421

   D $200,000

2   **What does the Miller-Orr model suggest is the spread between the upper and lower limits of cash levels that the Western division should maintain?**

   A $1,123

   B $8,028

   C $21,489

   D $153,569

3   **What will be the Southern division's cash receipts from sales in Month 5?**

   A $211,200

   B $248,400

   C $292,800

   D $346,800

4   **It is important to distinguish between a cash budget and a cash forecast. What is the validity of the following statements?**

Statement 1: A cash forecast is an estimate of cash receipts and payments for a future period under existing conditions before taking account of possible actions to modify cash flows, raise new capital, or invest surplus funds.

Statement 2: A cash budget is a commitment to a plan for cash receipts and payments for a future period after taking any action necessary to bring the preliminary cash forecast into conformity with the overall plan of the business.

A   Both statements are true

B   Both statements are false

C   Statement 1 only is true

D   Statement 2 only is true

11.1 THE ECONOMIC ENVIRONMENT FOR BUSINESS

LEARNING SUMMARY

After studying this section you should be able to:

- identify and explain the main macroeconomic policy targets

- define and discuss the role of fiscal, monetary, interest rate and exchange rate policies in achieving macroeconomic policy targets

- explain how government economic policy interacts with planning and decision making in business

- explain the need for and the interaction with planning and decision making in business of competition policy, government assistance for business, green policies and corporate governance regulation.

Macroeconomic policy

KEY POINT Macroeconomic policy is the management of the economy by government in such a way as to influence the performance and behaviour of the economy as a whole.

The principle objectives are set to satisfy key stakeholders, such as:

full employment of resources	full and stable employment
price stability	little or no inflation
economic growth	improving living standards
balance of payments equilibrium	ratio of imports to exports
an appropriate distribution of income and wealth	dependent on the prevailing political view

Pursuing all of these objectives may lead to potential conflict and trade-offs, for example:

full employment versus price stability	┈┈⟶	at full employment levels there is no room for the supply of goods and services to grow further
		if demand for products increases, then without extra supply being available, prices will rise

economic growth versus balance of payments	┈┈⟶	if the economy grows rapidly, it can take a while for suppliers to increase their productivity to match this growth
		the growth will come from imports in the meantime, leading to a deficit in the balance of payments

Monetary policy

The impact of monetary policy on business decision making:

The factors affected are:	Control of the money supply means:	Increasing interest rates means:
availability of finance	credit restrictions mean small businesses can struggle to raise funds	
cost of finance	reduced supply pushes up the cost of funds and discourages business expansion	shareholders require higher returns to make investing in shares worthwhile compared to interest earning investments without an increase in return, the share price falls
level of consumer demand	too difficult to raise funds to spend	saving becomes more attractive borrowing to spend is less attractive
exchange rates		high interest rates attract foreign investment and leads to a short-term increase in exchange rates (increased demand for currency) exports become more expensive imports become cheaper

All the above factors also influence inflation, which has a significant impact on business cash flows and profits. Inflation may be:

demand-pull inflation – due to excess demand	┄┄┄▶	for example, if interest rates are lowered, people are encouraged to spend rather than save the increased demand for products and services may not be met quickly with an increased supply and in the meantime prices will rise
cost-push inflation – due to higher costs	┄┄┄▶	for example, lowering interest rates can lead a decrease in the local exchange rate this can mean that imports become more expensive, pushing production costs up and leading to suppliers increasing prices to maintain profit

Fiscal policy

KEY POINT Fiscal policy is the manipulation of the government budget in order to influence the level of **aggregate demand** and therefore the level of activity in the economy.

DEFINITION Aggregate demand - the total demand for goods and services in the economy.

Fiscal policy covers:

government spending	for example, on healthcare, benefits, construction, business investment
taxation	from individuals and businesses
government borrowing	the issue and repayment of government debt

The role of the government is to balance the budget. Expenditure by the government is financed either by taxation or borrowing.

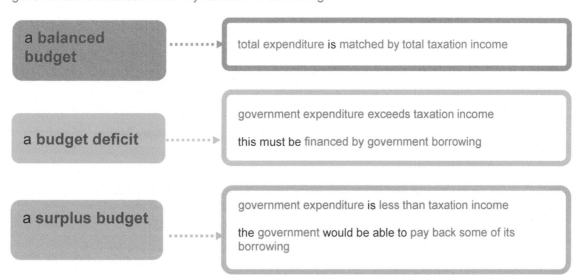

a balanced budget ·········▶ total expenditure is matched by total taxation income

a budget deficit ·········▶ government expenditure exceeds taxation income

this must be financed by government borrowing

a surplus budget ·········▶ government expenditure is less than taxation income

the government would be able to pay back some of its borrowing

Do you understand?

1   Which of the following statements is/are true?

Statement 1 – monetary policy seeks to regulate the economy by influencing such variables as the level of interest rates and conditions for availability of credit

Statement 2 – fiscal policy seeks to influence the economy by managing the amounts which the government spends and the amounts it collects through taxation

A   1 and 2

B   1

C   2

D   Neither

Government intervention and regulation

As well as the general policy measures to impact business operations, governments can also take more specific measures to regulate businesses:

competition policy	to prevent economic inefficiency, monopolies disadvantaging consumers and unfair pricing practises and to encourage innovation
provision of government assistance	to encourage economic growth through the use of grants and expert advice
green policies	to encourage firms to avoid negative externalities such as pollution
corporate governance guidelines	see below

Corporate governance

KEY POINT Corporate governance is defined as 'the system by which companies are directed and controlled' and covers issues such as ethics, risk management and stakeholder protection.

Corporate governance frameworks contain regulations on:

separation of the supervisory function and the management function	establishment of an audit committee and a remuneration committee
transparency in the recruitment and remuneration of the board	establishment of risk control procedures to monitor strategic, business and operational activities
appointment of non-executive directors (NEDs)	

1   **Which of the following is/are among the elements of fiscal policy?**

　　1　Government actions to raise or lower taxes

　　2　Government actions to raise or lower the size of the money supply

　　3　Government actions to raise or lower the amount it spends

　　A　1 only

　　B　1 and 3 only

　　C　2 and 3 only

　　D　1, 2 and 3

2   Governments have a number of economic targets as part of their fiscal policy.

　　Which of the following government actions relate predominantly to fiscal policy?

　　1　Decreasing interest rates in order to stimulate consumer spending

　　2　Reducing taxation while maintaining public spending

　　3　Using official foreign currency reserves to buy the domestic currency

　　4　Borrowing money from the capital markets and spending it on public works

　　A　1 only

　　B　1 and 3

　　C　2 and 4 only

　　D　2, 3 and 4

3   **Changes in monetary policy will influence which of the following factors?**

　　1　The level of exchange rates

　　2　The cost of finance

　　3　The level of consumer demand

　　4　The level of inflation

　　A　1 and 2 only

　　B　2 and 3 only

　　C　2, 3 and 4 only

　　D　1, 2 and 3 and 4

4 **Are the following statements are true or false?**

Statement	True	False
Demand-pull inflation might occur when excess aggregate monetary demand in the economy and hence demand for particular goods and services enable companies to raise prices and expand profit margins		
Cost-push inflation will occur when there are increases in production costs independent of the state of demand e.g. rising raw material costs or rising labour costs		

12.1 THE FINANCIAL SYSTEM

LEARNING SUMMARY

After studying this section you should be able to:

- identify the nature and role of money and capital markets, both nationally and internationally

- explain the functions of a stock market

- explain the role of financial intermediaries

- explain the nature and features of different securities in relation to the risk/return trade off

- explain the characteristics and role of the principal money market instruments

- explain the role of the treasury function.

KEY POINT The financial system channels funds from lenders to borrowers, provides a mechanism for payments, creates liquidity and money, provides financial services such as insurance and pensions, and offers facilities to manage investment portfolios.

It is a term which covers:

	for example:
financial markets	stock exchanges, money markets
financial institutions	banks, building societies, insurance companies and pension funds
financial securities	mortgages, bonds, bills and equity shares

Money and capital markets

KEY POINT Financial markets are mechanisms where those requiring finance (deficit units) can get in touch with those able to supply it (surplus units).

There are two main types of financial market:

money markets
deal in short-term funds (<1 year) and transactions

············▶

provide short-term liquidity to companies, banks and the public sector, for example:

- loans, factoring and commercial papers for companies
- inter-bank markets for banks and building societies
- loans to local government authorities

| **capital markets**
deal in longer-term finance, mainly via a stock exchange | ········▷ | which deal mainly in:

• public sector and foreign stocks
• company securities (shares and corporate bonds)
• eurobonds (bonds issued in a currency other than that of the national currency of the issuing company) |

Within money and capital markets are:

primary markets – which deal in the issue of new loanable funds	they provide a focal point for borrowers and lenders to meet
secondary markets – second-hand trading in securities, after having first been issued on the primary market	this market helps investors achieve: diversification – investing in a wide range of enterprises risk shifting – the choice of security gives investors a choice of the degree of risk hedging – taking out counterbalancing contracts to offset existing risks arbitrage – the process of buying a security at a low price in one market and simultaneously selling in another market to make a profit

KEY POINT An international financial market exists where domestic funds are supplied to a foreign user or foreign funds are supplied to a domestic user. The currencies need not be those of either the lender or the borrower.

The stock market

The role of the stock market is to:

facilitate trade in stocks such as:

issued shares of public companies

corporate bonds

government bonds

local authority loans

allocate capital to industry - share prices of attractive companies rise making it easier for them to raise cheap capital

determine a fair price for the assets traded

Speculative trading on the market can perform the following functions:

• smoothing price fluctuations

• ensuring shares are readily marketable

Market-makers are people who maintain stocks of securities in a number of quoted companies, they:

continually quote prices for buying and for selling the securities (bid and offer prices)

generate income by the profits they make from the difference (or 'spread') between the bid and offer prices

The syllabus does not require you to have any detailed knowledge of any specific country's stock market.

The role of financial institutions

There are three choices open to the end-users of the financial system:

lenders and borrowers contact each other directly ┄┄┄► this can be inefficient, risky and costly

lenders and borrowers use an organised financial market ┄┄┄► for example, purchase bonds from a company (lend money to the company), redeem company bonds or trade bonds to another investor

lenders and borrowers use financial institutions as intermediaries ┄┄┄► intermediation refers to the process whereby potential borrowers are brought together with potential lenders by a third party, the intermediary

financial intermediaries have a number of important roles:

- risk reduction - reducing the risk of a single default by lending to a wide variety of individuals and businesses
- aggregation - pooling small deposits to enable larger advances to be made
- maturity transformation -satisfying the different timescale needs of lenders (generally shorter) and borrowers (generally longer)
- financial intermediation - bringing together lenders and borrowers

for example, a lender obtains an asset which cannot usually be traded but only returned to the intermediary, this may be in the form of a bank deposit account or pension fund rights

intermediaries include:

- clearing banks
- insurance companies
- investment and unit trusts
- investment/merchant banks
- pension funds
- finance houses
- leasing companies
- factors
- savings banks and building societies

Money market instruments

KEY POINT A money market instrument is any type of security that is traded in the money market.

A financial manager will need to understand the characteristics of the following money market instruments:

coupon bearing securities	a fixed maturity and a specified rate of interest
certificates of deposit (CDs)	evidence of a deposit with an issuing bank
sale and repurchase agreements (repos)	an agreement to buy back later at a higher price
discount instruments	**issued at a discounted rate with fixed interest**
treasury bills	issued by governments
commercial bills	issued by large corporations
commercial paper	unsecured, with maturity between seven and forty five days
banker's acceptances	promised future payment

derivatives	contracts that give the right to buy and sell a quantity of an asset (for example, tea or shares)
forward rate agreements (FRAs) interest rate futures and options	a future price is fixed
caps and floors	the interest rate is capped at a certain level
interest rate swaps	an agreement to swap one stream of interest rates for another
swaptions	an option giving the right but not the obligation to engage in a swap.

The role of the treasury function

The treasury function of a firm usually has the following roles:

short-term management of resources	→	• short-term cash management – lending or borrowing funds as required • currency management
long-term maximisation of shareholder wealth	→	• raising long-term finance - including equity strategy, the management of debt capacity and the debt/equity structure • investment decisions - including investment appraisal, the review of acquisitions and divestments and the defence from takeover • dividend policy
risk management	→	• assessing risk exposure • interest rate risk management • hedging of foreign exchange risk

The corporate treasurer in an international group of companies will need to deal with the following specific functions:

setting transfer prices to reduce the overall tax bill (subject to local laws)

deciding currency exposure policies and procedures

transferring cash across international borders

devising investment strategies for short-term funds, from the range of international money markets and international marketable securities

netting and matching currency obligations

A company must choose between having its treasury management:

centralised - each operating company holds minimum cash and transfers surpluses to the centralised treasury department	decentralised - each operating company is responsible for its own treasury operations
avoids duplication of skills funding can be arranged in bulk, which is cheaper more effective foreign currency management netting off surpluses and deficits in same currency means less need for overdraft and incidence of bank charges	greater autonomy and motivation in operating companies better feel for local conditions and quicker response to developments

Do you understand?

1 Which of the following statements is correct?

    A   Money markets are markets for long term capital

    B   Capital markets are markets for short term capital

    C   Primary markets enable existing investors to sell their investments

    D   A financial intermediary links those with surplus funds to those with fund deficits

2 A large organisation will have a treasury department to manage liquidity, short term investment, borrowings, foreign exchange and other specialised areas.

Which of the following is not an advantage of having a centralised treasury department?

    A   Greater autonomy can be given to subsidiaries and divisions

    B   No need for treasury skills to be duplicated throughout the group

    C   Necessary borrowings can be arranged in bulk, at lower interest rates than for smaller borrowings

    D   The group's currency risk can be managed more effectively as the overall exposure to the group can be appreciated

2 A.

1 D.

1 Indicate whether the following statements are true or false

Statement	True	False
Coupon bearing securities have a fixed maturity and a specified rate of interest		
In the discount market, funds are raised by issuing bills at a discount to their eventual redemption or maturity value		

2 Which of the following are money market instruments?

1 Certificates of deposit

2 Corporate bonds

3 Commercial paper

4 Treasury bills

A 1, 2 and 4 only

B 1 and 3 only

C 1, 3 and 4 only

D 1, 2 and 3 and 4

3 Which THREE of the following are common roles of the treasury function within a firm?

A Short-term management of resources

B Long-term maximisation of shareholder wealth

C Long-term maximisation of market share

D Risk management

4 Which of the following is a difference between primary and secondary capital markets?

A Primary capital markets relate to the sale of new securities, while secondary capital markets are where securities trade after their initial offering

B Both primary and secondary capital markets relate to where securities are traded after their initial offering

C Both primary and secondary capital markets relate to the sale of new securities

D Primary markets are where stocks trade and secondary markets are where loan notes trade

13 Foreign exchange risk

The following topics are covered in this chapter:
- Foreign currency risk
- Exchange rate differences and interest rate fluctuations
- Hedging techniques for foreign currency risk

13.1 FOREIGN CURRENCY RISK

LEARNING SUMMARY

After studying this section you should be able to:

- describe and discuss transaction, economic and translation risk.

KEY POINT Foreign currency risk arises for companies that trade internationally.

Exchange rate systems

Floating exchange rates	The authorities allow the forces of supply and demand to continuously change the exchange rates without intervention.
	Increased demand for a currency or a shortage of supply would cause its price (rate) to rise and vice versa.
	The future value of a currency against other currencies is uncertain.
	The value of foreign trades will be affected.
	The world's leading currencies such as the US dollar, Japanese Yen, British pound and the European Euro float against each other.
Fixed exchange rates	Where a government uses monetary policy and other methods to hold the rate steady.
Freely floating exchange rates	There is no intervention by governments.
Managed floating exchange rates	Intervention to keep the value within a range.

Depreciation and appreciation of a currency

If a **currency depreciates** its **price (exchange rate) has fallen.** ....▶ More of it would be needed to purchase another currency and more of it could be bought with another currency.

If a **currency appreciates** its **price (exchange rate) has risen.** ....▶ Less of it would be needed to purchase another currency and less of it could be bought with another currency.

If one currency appreciates then another currency depreciates, for example:

$$\$1.50 = £1 \quad \rightarrow \quad \$1.60 = £1$$

the £ has appreciated (can now buy $1.60 instead of $1.50 with £1) and the $ has depreciated (it takes $1.60 instead of $1.50 to buy £1)

Types of foreign currency risk

DEFINITION A **transaction risk** is the risk of an exchange rate changing between the transaction date and the subsequent settlement date, i.e. it is the gain or loss arising on currency conversion.

A transaction risk arises on any future transaction involving conversion of cash between two currencies.

The most common area where transaction risk is experienced relates to imports and exports.

A firm may decide to hedge – take action to minimise – the risk, if it is:

a material amount

over a material time period

thought likely exchange rates will change significantly

For example:

On 1 Sep, a US company enters into a contract with a customer for which €100,000 is due to be received in 6 months.

The exchange rate on the date the contract is entered into is €0.93 = $1. Calculate the change in $ received compared to 1 Sep if the exchange rate moves to:

(1)   €0.97 = $1
(2)   €0.89 = $1

$ received at rate on 1 Sep = €100,000/0.93 = $107,527

(1) if rate moves to €0.97 = $1, $ received = €100,000/0.97 = $103,093, a loss of $4,434 compared to 1 Sep

(2) if rate moves to €0.89 = $1, $ received = €100,000/0.89 = $112,360, a gain of $4,833 compared to 1 Sep.

DEFINITION An **economic risk** is the variation in the value of the business (i.e. the present value of future cash flows) due to unexpected changes in exchange rates. It is the long-term version of transaction risk.

For an export company it could occur because:

The home currency strengthens against the currency in which it trades.

When the exporter receives the foreign currency from its customers, it must convert it to the home currency, which is now more expensive, meaning the exporter gets less for each transaction.

If the exporter invoices in its home currency it is still worse off as customers will need to buy the strong currency to pay the invoices and will be put off by the rising exchange rate.

A competitor's home currency weakens against the currency in which it trades.

The competitor company is now getting more of its home currency for the same invoices and may be able to lower its prices, making it more competitive than the home export company.

If both companies invoice in their home currencies then customers will prefer the supplier with the weaker currency.

Companies may choose to diversify their business internationally so that the company is not overexposed to any one economy in particular.

> **For example:**
> A US exporter sells one product in the UK on a cost-plus basis and invoices in £ to remain competitive in the UK market. The selling price in £ is based on costs of $125 plus a mark-up of 5% to give a sales price of $131.25. The current exchange rate is £0.81 = $1
>
> Does the exporter still make a profit on the goods if the exchange rate moves to £0.87 = $1?

Current invoice price: $131.25 × £0.81 = £106.31

If the exchange rate moves, £106.31 will be received and then converted into US$ at the new rate.

At the new rate, this would give £106.31/0.87 = $122.20.

With costs of $125, the exporter is no longer able to make a profit at the same sales price.

DEFINITION A **translation risk** is where the reported performance of an overseas subsidiary in home-based currency terms is distorted in financial statements because of a change in exchange rates. This is an accounting risk rather than a cash-based one.

13.2 EXCHANGE RATE DIFFERENCES AND INTEREST RATE FLUCTUATIONS

LEARNING SUMMARY

After studying this section you should be able to:

- describe the causes of exchange rate fluctuations
- forecast exchange rates.

The foreign exchange market

KEY POINT The foreign exchange market is an international market in foreign currencies. It is highly competitive and virtually no difference exists between the prices in one market (e.g. New York) and another (e.g. London).

Banks dealing in foreign currency quote two prices for an exchange rate:

| a lower 'bid' price | the bank sells low |
| a higher 'offer' price | the bank buys high |

DEFINITION The **spot market** is where you can buy and sell a currency now (immediate delivery), i.e. the spot rate of exchange is the exchange rate as of today.

DEFINITION The **forward market** is where you can buy and sell a currency at a fixed future date for a predetermined rate, by entering into a forward exchange contract.

> The PPPT and IRPT formulas are given in the exam.

The causes of exchange rate fluctuations

Purchasing power parity theory (PPPT)

formula to estimate expected future spot rates

=

$$S_1 = S_0 \times \frac{(1 + h_c)}{(1 + h_b)}$$

S_0 = current spot
S_1 = expected future spot
h_b = inflation rate in country for which the spot is quoted (base currency)
h_c = inflation rate in the other country (counter currency)

The rate of exchange between two currencies depends on the relative inflation rates within the respective countries.

The country with the higher inflation rate will be subject to a depreciation of its currency.

For example, the current exchange rate between Euros and US$ is €0.93 = $1.
If inflation in the Eurozone is anticipated to be 2.5% over the next year and in the US will be 3%, the future spot rate in a year's time is:

$S_1 = 0.93 \times 1.025/1.03 = €0.925 = 1

Interest rate parity theory (IRPT)

formula to estimate expected forward rates

=

$$F_0 = S_0 \times \frac{(1 + i_c)}{(1 + i_b)}$$

S_0 = current spot
F_0 = forward rate
i_b = interest rate for base currency
i_c = interest rate for counter currency

the difference between the spot and the forward exchange rates is equal to the differential between interest rates available in the two countries

the country with the higher interest rate will see the forward rate for its currency subject to depreciation

for example, the current exchange rate between Euros and US$ is €0.93 = $1
if interest in the Eurozone is anticipated to be 5% over the next year and in the US will be 6%, the forward rate for delivery in a year's time is:

$F_0 = 0.93 \times 1.05/1.06 = €0.921 = 1

Limitations of purchasing power parity theory	Limitations of interest rate parity theory
the future inflation rates are estimates	government controls on capital markets
the market is dominated by speculative transactions	controls on currency trading
government may intervene to manage exchange rates	intervention in foreign exchange markets

Do you understand?

1   The spot exchange rate is:

   A   the rate for exchanging one currency for another for immediate delivery

   B   the rate today for exchanging one currency for another at a specified future date

   C   the rate today for exchanging one currency for another at a specific location on a specified future date

   D   the rate today for exchange one currency for another at a specific location for immediate delivery

1. A

13.3 HEDGING TECHNIQUES FOR FOREIGN CURRENCY RISK

LEARNING SUMMARY

After studying this section you should be able to:

- discuss and apply traditional methods of foreign currency risk management

- compare and evaluate traditional methods of foreign currency risk management.

KEY POINT Taking measures to eliminate or reduce a risk is called hedging the risk or hedging the exposure.

Practical approaches to dealing with risk are:

Deal in home currency	transfers risk to the other party
	but, may not be commercially acceptable
Do nothing	works for small occasional transactions
Leading	ask for immediate payment, if it is anticipated that there will be an adverse movement in exchange rates
Lagging	delay payments due, if it is anticipated that there will be favourable movement in exchange rates
Matching receipts and payments of the same foreign currency	net off to reduce exposure
Netting	inter-company balances are netted off before payment

Open a foreign currency bank accounts	if there are lots of transactions in that currency
Matching assets and liabilities	for example, pay for a foreign asset with a foreign currency loan

Forward exchange contracts

DEFINITION A **forward exchange contract** is a binding contract which specifies in advance the rate at which a specified currency will be bought and sold at a specified future time.

Advantages	Disadvantages
flexibility on amount and date	contractual commitment
straightforward	no opportunity to benefit from favourable rate movements

Do you understand?

1   A forward exchange contract is:

  i   an immediately firm and binding contract

  ii   is for the purchase or sale of a specified quantity of a stated foreign currency

  iii   is at a rate of exchange fixed at the time the contract is made

  iv   for performance at a future time which is agreed when making the contract

  A   (i) and (ii) only

  B   (i) and (iv) only

  C   (ii) and (iii) only

  D   all of them

1 D.

Money market hedges

Hedging a payment - steps	Hedging a receipt - steps
1 Divide the foreign currency payment amount by (1 plus the foreign currency deposit rate for the time period in question).	**1** Divide the foreign currency receipt amount by (1 plus the foreign currency borrowing rate for the time period in question).
2 Take the figure calculated and translate it to the home currency at the spot rate.	**2** Take the figure calculated and translate it to the home currency at the spot rate.
3 Take the figure calculated and multiply it by (1 plus the home currency borrowing rate for the time period in the question).	**3** Take the figure calculated and multiply it by (1 plus the home currency deposit rate for the time period in the question).

Foreign currency derivatives

Currency futures

······▶

- are like a forward in that they fix the foreign currency rate and are binding
- are tradable on futures exchanges (the futures contract is separate from the underlying currency exchange)
- are settled on three monthly cycles (unlike forwards which can be for any date)
- are for standardised amounts (unlike forwards which can be for any amount)
- are priced at the exchange rate specified in the contract

Currency options - give the right, but not the obligation to buy or sell currency at some point in the future at a predetermined rate

······▶

a company will therefore:
- exercise the option if it is in its interests to do so (if the rate has moved unfavourably), or
- let the option lapse (if the rate has moved favourably or if there is no longer a need to exchange currency)
- options provide extra flexibility – the opportunity to take advantage of favourable rate movements, but they come with a cost – a premium paid up front which is spent whether the option is exercised or not.

Options may be:
- put – the right to sell currency at a particular rate
- call – the right to buy currency at a particular rate

Do you understand?

1   A company whose home currency is the dollar ($) expects to receive 500,000 pesos in six months' time from a customer in a foreign country. The following interest rates and exchange rates are available to the company:

Spot rate   15.00 peso per $

Six month forward rate   15.30 peso per $

	Home country	Foreign country
Borrowing interest rate	4% per year	8% per year
Deposit interest rate	3% per year	6% per year

Working to the nearest $100, what is the six month dollar value of the expected receipt using a money market hedge?

A $32,500

B $33,700

C $31,800

D $31,900

1. A.

Divide the foreign currency receipt amount by (1 plus the foreign currency borrowing rate for the time period in question) (500,000/1.04 = 480,769).

Take the figure calculated and translate it to the home currency at the spot rate (480,769/15 = 32,051).

Take the figure calculated and multiply it by (1 plus the home currency deposit rate for the time period in the question) (32,051 × 1.015 = 32,532).

New Co is a UK-based company which has the following expected transactions.

One month: Expected receipt of $240,000

One month: Expected payment of $140,000

Three months: Expected receipts of $300,000

The finance manager has collected the following information:

Spot rate ($ per £): 1.7820 ± 0.0002

One month forward rate ($ per £): 1.7829 ± 0.0003

Three months forward rate ($ per £): 1.7846 ± 0.0004

Money market rates for New Co:

	Borrowing	Deposit
One year sterling interest rate:	4.9%	4.6%
One year dollar interest rate:	5.4%	5.1%

Assume that it is now 1 April.

Required:

1 **Discuss the differences between transaction risk, translation risk and economic risk.**

2 **Calculate the expected sterling receipts in one month and in three months using the forward market.**

3 **Calculate the expected sterling receipts in three months using a money-market hedge and recommend whether a forward market hedge or a money market hedge should be used.**

4 **Discuss how sterling currency futures contracts could be used to hedge the three-month dollar receipt.**

14 Interest rate risk

The following topics are covered in this chapter:
- Interest rate exposure and fluctuations
- Hedging interest rate risk

14.1 INTEREST RATE EXPOSURE AND FLUCTUATIONS

LEARNING SUMMARY

After studying this section you should be able to:

- describe and discuss different types of interest risk
- describe the causes of interest rate fluctuations.

KEY POINT Financial managers face risk from changes in interest rates. Even if a company has matched its variable rate loans against its variable rate deposits there may still be **basis risk** if the rates on each are not calculated in the same way.

DEFINITION **Basis risk** is the risk that investments which, in theory, should offset each other in terms of changing values, do not do so.

The types of risk financial managers may face may be with:

Existing loans	variable rate – risk that interest rates will rise
	fixed rate – risk that interest rates will fall (and so the company can't take advantage of the fall)
Existing deposits	variable rate – risk that interest rates will fall
	fixed rate – risk that interest rates will rise (and so the company can't take advantage of the rise)
Future loans and deposits	the risk that interest rates will change before the loan or deposit contract is entered into

Gap exposure

KEY POINT The degree to which a firm is exposed to interest rate risk can be identified through gap analysis. This uses the principle of grouping together assets and liabilities that are affected by interest rate changes according to their maturity dates.

A negative gap
- Interest-sensitive liabilities maturing at a certain time are greater than interest-sensitive assets maturing at the same time.
- Exposure to rising interest rates

A positive gap
- Interest-sensitive liabilities maturing at a certain time are less than interest-sensitive assets maturing at the same time.
- Exposure to falling interest rates.

Why interest rates fluctuate

The yield curve:

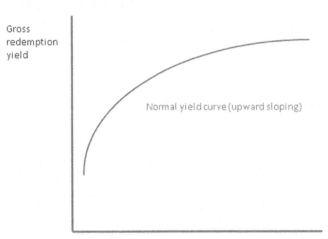

There are three types of yield curve:

Normal yield curve	longer maturity bonds have a higher yield due to the risks associated with time.
Inverted yield curve	shorter-term yields are higher than longer-term ones, which can be a sign of an upcoming recession.
Flat (or humped) yield curve	the shorter and longer-term yields are very close to each other, which is also a predictor of an economic transition.

The shape of the yield curve at any point in time is the result of the three following theories acting together:

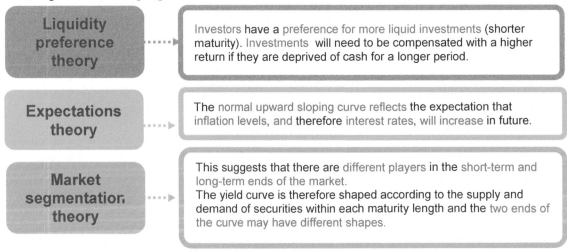

Financial managers should inspect the shape of the curve when deciding on the term of borrowings or deposits. For example, a normal upward sloping yield curve suggests that interest rates may rise in the future:

- avoid borrowing on long-term variable rates

- choose to borrow on short-term variable or long-term fixed rates instead.

Do you understand?

1   An inverse yield curve is a possible indication of:

    A   an expected rise in interest rates

    B   an expected fall in interest rates

    C   higher than expected inflation

    D   lower than expected inflation

1. C.

14.2 HEDGING INTEREST RATE RISK

LEARNING SUMMARY

After studying this section you should be able to:

- discuss and apply traditional methods of interest rate risk management

- identify the main types of interest rate derivatives used to hedge interest rate risk and explain how they are used.

Forward rate agreements (FRAs)

KEY POINT The aim of a forward rate agreement is to lock the company into a target interest rate, and hedge both adverse and favourable interest rate movements.

The company enters into a normal loan and separately into a forward rate agreement with a bank:

The company pays interest on the loan in the normal way.

If the interest rate paid is greater than the agreed forward rate, the bank pays the difference to the company.

If the interest rate paid is less than the agreed forward rate, the company pays the difference to the bank.

For example:

A company will need to borrow €55 million in 3 months' time for 6 months. A 3–9 FRA is available at 6.6% – 6.3% per annum.

The interest payable if the interest rate moves to 7% per annum by the date of the borrowing, is:

the borrowing rate is the higher of the spread so the rate will be effectively fixed at 6.6%.

Interest paid on underlying borrowing: €55m × 7% × 6/12 = €1,925,000.
As the interest rate is higher than the FRA rate, the FRA bank must pay the difference over to the company: €55m × (7% – 6.6%) × 6/12 = €110,000.

net interest paid = €1,925,000 – €110,000 = €1,815,000

Do you understand?

1   It is 30 June and Company F will need a $10 million six month rate loan from 1 October. Company F wants to hedge using a forward rate agreement (FRA). The relevant FRA rate is 6% on 30 June.

What is the interest payable/receivable via the FRA contract if in six months' time the market rate is 9%?

A $150,000 receivable

B $150,000 payable

C $450,000 receivable

D $450,000 payable

1   A. $10 million x (0.09 − 0.06) x 6/12 = $150,000 receivable.

Interest rate guarantees (IRGs)

KEY POINT An interest rate guarantee is an option on a forward rate agreement. It allows the company a period of time during which it has the option to buy a forward rate agreement at a set price.

Interest rate guarantees protect a company from adverse movements and allow it to take advantage of favourable movements:

| if there is an **adverse movement** | ┄┄┄► | exercise the option to protect |

| if there is a **favourable movement** | ┄┄┄► | allow the option to lapse |

Interest rate guarantees are more expensive than forward rate agreements, due to their flexibility.

Interest rate futures (IRFs)

KEY POINT Interest rate futures lock a company into the effective interest rate, and hedge both adverse and favourable interest rate movements.

A futures contract is a promise, for example:

*   If you sell a futures contract, you have a contract to borrow money – what you are selling is the promise to make interest payments:

If you know you will need a loan in the future, sell futures contracts now.

When the borrowing is needed, enter into the loan in the normal way. This is a separate contract to the futures contract.

Also at this point, close out the futures contract, by buying it back.

The loan and the buying back of the futures contracts effectively cancel each other out.

Interest rate changes since the point at which the futures contracts were initially sold have no effect.

Perform the opposite futures transactions for a deposit - buy up front and sell on close out.

Basis risk

- Basis risk arises because the futures price only matches the spot interest rate on the exact date of close out - the difference on any other date is the basis.

- Imperfect hedges also occur because the contracts are standardised in value and therefore may not cover the exact deposit or loan value.

Options	Borrowers may additionally buy options on futures contracts. As with any option, it gives the chance to protect against downside risk by exercising the option and to take advantage of favourable movements by letting the option lapse.
Interest rate caps, floors and collars	Borrowers/investors can use interest rate options to set: - maximum rates - interest rate cap - minimum rates - interest rate floor - a confined range of rates - interest rate collar
Swaps	An interest rate swap is where the parties agree to swap a floating (variable) stream of interest payments for a fixed stream of interest payments and vice versa. - A company may swap from fixed to floating because it believes interest rates will move favourably in future. - A company may swap from floating to fixed because it wants certainty about its cash payments or because it believes that interest rates will move adversely in future. Currency swaps are also available whereby debt in different currencies is swapped.

Do you understand?

1   An interest rate swap:

    A   allows the company a period of time during which it has the option to buy a forward rate agreement at a set price

    B   locks the company into an effective interest rate

    C   is an agreement where the parties to the agreement exchange interest rate commitments

    D   involves the exchange of principle

1 C.

Exam style questions

1   **The following statements refer to interest rate risk. Are each of the following statements true or false?**

Statement 1: The aim of a forward rate agreement (FRA) is to lock the company into a target interest rate and hedge both adverse and favourable interest rate movements.

Statement 2: An interest rate guarantees (IRG) is more expensive than an FRA as one has to pay for the flexibility to be able to take advantage of favourable interest rate movements.

	Statement 1	Statement 2
A	True	True
B	False	True
C	True	False
D	False	False

2   **The following statements refer to interest rate futures. Are each of the following statements true or false?**

Statement 1: If you sell a futures contract you have a contract to lend money.

Statement 2: Each contract is for a standardised amount with a set maturity date. A whole number of contracts must be dealt with.

	Statement 1	Statement 2
A	True	True
B	False	True
C	True	False
D	False	False

3   The shape of the yield curve at any point in time is the result of three theories acting together.

Which of the following theories does NOT influence the yield curve?

A   Liquidity preference theory

B   Expectations theory

C   Flat yield theory

D   Market segmentation theory

4   **Which of the following statements is correct?**

A   Governments may choose to raise interest rates so that the level of general expenditure in the economy will increase

B   The normal yield curve slopes upward to reflect increasing compensation to investors for being unable to use their cash now

C   The yield on long-term loan notes is lower than the yield on short-term loan notes because long-term debt is less risky for a company than short-term debt

D   Expectations theory states that future interest rates reflect expectations of future inflation rate movements

15 Sources of finance

The following topics are covered in this chapter:

- Risk versus return
- Sources of finance for business
- Finance for small and medium businesses
- Islamic finance

15.1 RISK VERSUS RETURN

LEARNING SUMMARY

After studying this section you should be able to:

- explain the relationship between risk and return.

The need for finance

KEY POINT Firms need finance to provide working capital and invest in non-current assets.

The criteria for choosing a source of finance:

Cost	Debt finance is usually cheaper than equity finance.
Duration	Long-term finance is usually more expensive but more secure than short-term.
Term structure of interest rates	Short-term finance is usually cheaper, but not always.
Gearing	The ratio of debt to equity finance. Adding debt is usually cheaper than equity, but high gearing is risky.
Accessibility	not all sources are available to all firms.

The relationship between risk and return

KEY POINT Investment risk arises because returns are variable and uncertain. An increase in risk generally requires an increase in expected returns.

Each time an investor demands a higher return on the finance they have provided, this is reflected in a higher cost of that finance to the company.

15.2 SOURCES OF FINANCE FOR BUSINESS

LEARNING SUMMARY

After studying this section you should be able to:

- identify and discuss the range of short-term sources of finance available to business

- identify and discuss methods of raising equity finance

- identify and discuss the range of long-term sources of finance available to business.

Short-term sources of finance

bank overdrafts	flexible, only used when needed
bank loans	secure, may only be available if a business has assets to use as security
better management of working capital	profitability versus liquidity decisions
leasing	spreading the cost of the asset
sale and leaseback	generates cash to be used for other purposes

Long-term sources of finance - equity

KEY POINT Equity finance is the investment in a company by the ordinary shareholder, represented by the issued ordinary share capital plus reserves.

DEFINITION Equity shareholders (ordinary shareholders) are the owners of the business and exercise ultimate control through their voting rights.

Note - preference shares are not considered part of equity.

The main sources of equity finance are:

internally generated funds

- retained earnings which have not already been paid out as dividends or used for prior investment
- quick and cheap source of finance, if available

rights issues

- the issue of new shares to existing shareholders in proportion to their existing shareholdings, at a discount to the current market value
- more expensive than internally generated funds, but cheaper than a new issue
- shareholders can sell their rights instead of taking them up.
- issuing new shares at a discount will cause the share price to fall:

$$TERP = \frac{\text{market value of shares already in issue} + \text{proceeds from new share issue}}{\text{number of shares in issue after the rights issue}}$$

TERP = theoretical ex-rights price

new external share issues

- expensive
- may fail
- may require business to become quoted, where there are stringent criteria to adhere to
- via placing, for example, enterprise investment scheme, public offer, fixed price offer, offer for sale by tender
- there will be dilution of control for existing shareholders

Do you understand?

1   Company S has announced a 1 for 5 rights issue at a subscription price of $2.30. The current cum-rights price of the shares is $3.35.

What is the new ex-dividend market value of the shares?

A $3.18

B $3.81

C $2.97

D $2.48

The value of a right

KEY POINT   As a rights issue gives the opportunity to buy shares at a discount, the right itself has value and can be sold on.

value of a right =

TERP – issue (subscription) price

value of a right per existing share =

(TERP – issue price)/no. of shares needed to obtain a right

For example:
a company has an issued share capital of 5 million shares each priced at $10.50, makes a rights issue of one new share for every 4 currently in issue the issue price is $9.50 and the TERP is $10.30

the value of a right and the value of a right per existing share is:

value of a right = $10.30 – $9.50 = $0.80

value of a right per existing share = $0.80/(4/1) = $0.20

The shareholder's options with a rights issue are to:

take up the rights by buying the specified proportion of shares at the price offered

renounce the rights and sell them in the market

renounce part of the rights and take up the remainder

do nothing - will lose wealth as shares held will fall in value to the TERP

Long-term sources of finance - debt

The features of bonds are:

traded on stock markets

usually denominated in blocks of $100 nominal value

may be secured or unsecured

security may come in the form of a fixed charge over specific assets, or a floating charge over all assets, or a category of assets

may be redeemable or irredeemable

if redeemable the repayment date will be specified in the terms of the bond

Characteristics of long-term debt:

Advantages

from the viewpoint of the investor, debt:
- is low risk

from the viewpoint of the company, debt:
- is cheap
- has predictable flows
- does not dilute control

These are key points for discussion in the exam.

Disadvantages

from the viewpoint of the investor, debt:
- has no voting rights

from the viewpoint of the company, debt:
- is inflexible
- increases risk at high levels of gearing
- must be repaid

Different types of bonds:

Deep discount	issued at a discount to nominal value and redeemable at par and above
Zero coupon	like deep discount but no interest is paid whilst in issue
Hybrids – convertibles	give the bond holder the right to convert (if they choose at the time) the debt into other securities, normally ordinary shares, at a future date
	converted at either a pre-determined price or ratio
	conversion premium occurs if the market value of the convertible stock is greater than the market value of the shares the stock can be converted into
	floor value is the minimum market price of the note, calculated as the present value of the future interest plus the present value of the cash redemption value

Hybrids – loan notes with warrants	give the bond holder the right to subscribe at a fixed future date for a certain number of ordinary shares at a predetermined price
	the loan notes are not converted, they remain in place after the subscription date
	can be used to make the debt more attractive and able to set a low coupon rate
	holder gets right to buy shares at an attractive price
	holder can sell on the warrants, effectively reducing the cost of purchasing the debt

KEY POINT Venture capital is the provision of risk-bearing capital, usually in the form of a participation in equity, to companies with high growth potential.

Venture capitalists provide start-up and late stage growth finance, usually for smaller firms and will often look for an exit route in the form of flotation of the company enabling them to sell their investment.

Do you understand?

1 Which of the following is a key feature of debt as a source of finance?

A Interest must be paid irrespective of the level of profits generated by the company

B Debt holders are repaid last in the case of a winding up of the company

C Debt holders hold full voting rights

D Debt holders suffer relatively high levels of risk, compared to providers of other sources of finance, and therefore debt attracts the highest return

1 A

15.3 FINANCE FOR SMALL AND MEDIUM ENTERPRISES

LEARNING SUMMARY

After studying this section you should be able to:

- describe the financing needs for small businesses

- describe the nature of the financing problem for small businesses in terms of the funding gap and the maturity gap.

Small and medium enterprises (SMEs) tend to be unquoted, and can have difficulty raising finance because they have a:

- small number of owners with limited capital available between them

- lack of business history or proven track record

- lower level of public scrutiny over accounts and records

The **funding gap**	unquoted SMEs may find they have an inability to raise funding without becoming quoted, this may be bridged by using: • business angels or venture capitalists • government assistance • supply chain financing, crowdfunding, or peer-to-peer funding

The **maturity gap**	SMEs may find it easier to obtain long-term finance secured against their assets than short or medium-term finance but, for short to medium-term assets, it would be preferable to raise short to medium-term finance to match the term of its assets against its liabilities and keep funding costs down the inability to do this is known as the maturity gap.

15.4 ISLAMIC FINANCE

LEARNING SUMMARY

After studying this section you should be able to:

- identify and discuss methods of raising short and long-term Islamic finance.

KEY POINT Islamic finance has the same purpose as other forms of business finance, except that it operates in accordance with the principles of Islamic law (Sharia).

The basic principles covered by Islamic finance include:

- sharing of profits and losses

- no interest (riba) allowed

- finance is restricted to transactions accepted by the Islamic faith, i.e. no investment in alcohol, gambling, etc.

DEFINITION **Riba** is the excess paid by the borrower over the original capital borrowed, the equivalent to interest on a loan.

KEY POINT Instead of interest being charged, returns are earned by channelling funds into an underlying investment activity, which will earn profit. The investor is rewarded by a share in that profit, after a management fee is deducted by the bank.

The main sources of finance within the Islamic banking model include:

Murabaha	trade credit	Mudaraba	equity finance
Ijara	lease finance	Musharaka	venture capital
Sukuk	debt finance		

Do you understand?

1   With reference to Islamic finance, the term Riba refers to:

     A   a form of equity where a partnership exists and profits and losses are shared

     B   the predetermined interest collected by a lender, which the lender receives over and above the principal amount that it has lent out

     C   a form of credit sale

     D   a form of lease

1   B.

1   Investing in a small or medium sized business (SME) is inherently
     more risky than investing in a larger company due to lack of business
     history and a lower level of public scrutiny over accounts and records.

     **What is the frequently used term to describe the difficulty SMEs
     can often face when raising finance?**

     A   Maturity gap

     B   Funding gap

     C   Duration gap

     D   Equity gap

2   **Company C has $5m of $0.50 nominal value ordinary shares in
     issue. It recently announced a 1 for 4 rights issue at $6 per
     share. Its share price on the announcement of the rights issue
     was $8 per share.**

     What is the theoretical value of a right per existing share?

     A $1.60

     B $0.40

     C $0.50

     D $1.50

3   **In relation to preference shares as a source of capital for a
     company, fill in the gaps below to complete the sentence.**

     Preference shares are a form of .... capital which carry .... risk
     from the company point of view than ordinary shares.

     Choose from the following:

     equity

     loan

     lower

     higher

16 Dividend policy

The following topics are covered in this chapter:

- Dividend policy theory

16.1 DIVIDEND POLICY THEORY

LEARNING SUMMARY

After studying this section you should be able to:

- explain the relationship between the dividend decision and the financing decision.

The dividend decision

Should an organisation pay out a regular dividend or use the cash to fund further investment?

There are three main theories concerning what impact a cut in the dividend will have on a company and its shareholders:

Dividend irrelevancy theory (Modigliani and Miller)	assumptions: • a perfect capital market exists • no transaction costs • no taxes or dividends, and capital gains are taxed in the same way theory: the **pattern of dividend pay-outs should be irrelevant**, as long as companies continue **to invest in positive net present value (NPV) projects**, the **wealth of the shareholders should increase whether or not the company makes a dividend payment in the year** Modigliani and Miller (M&M) suggested that **entities should focus on investment policy rather than dividend policy**, and that if investors required income, they could sell shares to 'manufacture' dividends

Residual theory	• this theory is closely related to M&Ms but **recognises the costs involved in raising new finance** • it argues that **dividends** themselves **are important,** but the **pattern** of them **is not** • only after a firm has invested in all positive NPV projects should a dividend be paid if there are any funds remaining

Dividend relevance	practical influences on dividend policy: • **dividend signalling** -reductions in dividends can convey 'bad news' to shareholders who aren't fully informed about why the dividend has been cut (a market imperfection) • **investor liquidity requirements** -a cut in a dividend or an unexpected dividend may conflict with investors' liquidity requirements • **clientele effect** -investors may have invested for a specific reason such as tax planning, as income tax and capital gains tax are taxed differently, a dividend policy change can affect the taxes incurred by investors as a result **companies tend to adopt a stable dividend policy** and keep shareholders informed of any changes

Other practical constraints are:

legal restrictions on dividend payments, such as:

rules as to distributable profits that prevent excess cash distributions

bond and loan agreements may contain covenants that restrict the amount of dividends a firm can pay

liquidity

the availability of cash must be considered, not just to fund the dividends, but also to fund the continuing working capital requirements

Alternatives to cash dividends are:

Share repurchase ···▶ buy back of shares, particularly if the amount of surplus cash available would distort normal dividend policy

Scrip dividends ···▶ allows shareholders to take their dividends in the form of new shares rather than cash

note – this is not a bonus (scrip) issue, which is a method of altering share capital without raising cash

Do you understand?

1 The 'dividends as residuals' view of dividend policy is best described as:

A dividends are paid if the company generates profits greater than the previous year

B the profits made by the division of a company in a particular country should be paid to shareholders of the same nationality

C dividends should amount to the entire annual profit less the amount paid in manager incentive schemes

D dividends should only be paid out of cash flow after the company has financed all of its positive net present value projects

2 A scrip dividend is:

A a dividend paid at a fixed percentage rate on the nominal value of shares

B a dividend paid at a fixed percentage rate on the market value of the shares on the date that the dividend is declared

C a dividend payment that takes the form of new shares instead of cash

D a cash dividend that is not fixed but is decided upon by the directors and approved by the shareholders

2. C
1. D

1   Which of the following is the best statement of the conclusion of Modigliani and Miller on the relevance of dividend policy?

A   All shareholders are indifferent between receiving dividend income and capital gains

B   Increase in retentions results in a higher growth rate

C   Discounting the dividends is not an appropriate way to value the firm's equity

D   The value of the shareholders' equity is determined solely by the firm's investment selection criteria

2   Which of the following statements is correct?

A   A bonus issue can be used to raise new equity finance

B   A share repurchase scheme can increase both earnings per share and gearing

C   Miller and Modigliani argued that the financing decision is more important than the dividend decision

D   Shareholders usually have the power to increase dividends at annual general meetings of a company

17 The cost of capital

The following topics are covered in this chapter:
- Estimating the cost of capital
- The capital asset pricing model

17.1 ESTIMATING THE COST OF CAPITAL

LEARNING SUMMARY

After studying this section you should be able to:

- estimate the cost of equity, including application of the dividend valuation model

- estimate the cost of debt, including preference shares, irredeemable debt, redeemable debt and convertible debt

- estimate the overall cost of capital, including the weighted average cost of capital

- describe the relative risk-return relationship and the relative costs of equity and debt.

Calculating the cost of capital

KEY POINT The discount rate used in investment appraisal, known as the cost of capital, represents the company's costs of long-term finance.

The costs of each source of finance will differ depending on the risk levels taken on by the investor in that finance.

If an investor takes on higher risk in their investment they will seek a higher return.

To calculate a cost of capital:

Identify the sources of finance used	Look for equity, preference share and debt sources, bearing in mind that there may be more than one debt source.
For each type calculate the cost	The cost of each source of finance can be equated with the return which the providers of finance (investors) are demanding on their investment. This return can be expressed as a percentage. To calculate the return being demanded, in a perfect market: **market value of investment = present value (PV) of expected future returns discounted at the investors' required rate of return.** This is the same as: **investors' required rate of return = internal rate of return (IRR) of investing at current market price and receiving the future expected returns.**
Calculate a weighted average of all the costs	The weighting will be the value (either book or market value) of each finance source.

> This is a key point for the exam.

Estimating the cost of equity – the dividend valuation model (DVM)

DVM with no growth in dividends

$$r_e = D/P_o$$

r_e = shareholders' required return, expressed as a decimal, or percentage
D = constant dividend from year 1 to infinity
P_o = ex div market price of a share (ex div = AFTER dividend paid)

ex div share price = cum div share price – dividend due

The value of r_e is equivalent to k_e (the cost of equity finance to the company).

In the exam, prices could be quoted e div or cur div.

For example,
Company X has paid a dividend of $0.25 per share for many years and expects to continue paying out at this level for the foreseeable future.
The company's current share price is $2.45.

The cost of equity using the dividend valuation model is:

$k_e = D/P_0$
$k_e = \$0.25/\$2.45 = 0.102$ or 10.2%

DVM with dividend growth at a fixed rate

$$r_e = \frac{D_0 (1 + g)}{P_0} + g \quad = \quad \frac{D_1}{P_0} + g$$

D_0 = current dividend
D_1 = dividend in 1 years' time
g = constant rate of growth in dividends

The first formula is given in the exam.

For example,
Company Y has just paid out a dividend of $0.45 per share and expects dividends to grow at a rate of 3% per annum for the foreseeable future.
The current share price is $3.50 per share.

The cost of equity using the dividend valuation model is:

$k_e = [D_0 (1 + g)/P_0] + g$
$k_e = [\$0.45 \times 1.03/\$3.50] + 0.03 = 0.162$ or 16.2%

Do you understand?

1   The shares of company B have a current market price of 74 cents each, ex div. It is expected that the dividend in one year's time will be 8 cents per share. The required rate of return is 16% per annum.

It is expected growth in future dividends is a constant annual percentage. What is the expected annual dividend growth?

A   0.4% per annum

B   3.5% per annum

C   3.8% per annum

D   5.2% per annum

1. D. $r_e = (D_1/P_0) + g$
$0.16 = (8/74) + g$
$g = 0.052$ or 5.2%

Estimating growth – past dividends

$$g = (D_0/D_n)^{1/n} ; 1$$

D_n = dividend n years ago
n = number of years of growth

For example,
a company's dividend just paid was **$0.63 per share. Six years ago the dividend was $0.50 per share.**

The annual growth rate in dividends is:

$g = (D_0/D_n)^{1/n} - 1$
$g = (\$0.63/\$0.50)^{1/6} - 1$
$g = 0.039$ or 3.9%

Estimating growth ; earnings retention model (Gordon's growth model)

$$g = br_e$$

b = earnings retention rate
r_e = accounting rate of return

Gordon's growth model formula is given in the exam.

For example,
an all equity financed company has made profits after taxation of **$15,000 for the year. It then pays out a dividend of $8,250. Opening capital was $50,000.**

Assuming the company's return on capital and its dividend pay-out ratio remains the same, the growth in dividends for next year is:

$g = b \times r_e$
b = earnings retention rate = ($15,000 − $8,250)/$15,000 = 0.45 (or 45%)
r_e = accounting rate of return = $15,000/$50,000 = 0.3 (or 30%)
$g = 0.45 \times 0.3 = 0.135$ or 13.5%

Estimating the cost of preference shares

Cost of the preference share (k_p) $k_p = D/P_o$

Estimating the cost of debt

Debt terminology:

The terms loan notes, bonds, loan stock and marketable debt are used interchangeably

Gilts are debts issued by the government.

Irredeemable debt – the company does not intend to repay the principle, but will pay interest forever.

Redeemable debt – the company will pay interest for a number of years, and then repay the principal.

Convertible debt – may be later converted to equity.

Ex-interest – after interest payment.

Cum-interest – before interest payment.

- Debt is always quoted in $100 nominal blocks.

- Interest paid on the debt is stated as a percentage of nominal value, called the coupon rate.

Pre-tax - the required return of the debt holder (investor)	K_d
Post tax - the cost of the debt to the company	$K_d(1-T)$ T = the rate of corporation tax

Cost of irredeemable debt

$$k_d = \frac{I}{MV} \qquad `k_d(1-T)' = \frac{I(1-T)}{MV}$$

I = annual interest starting in one year's time
MV = ex-interest market price of the loan note

For example,
company B has in issue 6% irredeemable debt quoted at $105 (ex-interest). The corporation tax rate is 30%.

The return required by the debt providers is:

$K_d = I/MV$
$K_d = (\$100 \times 6\%)/\$105 = 0.057$ or 5.7%

the cost of debt to company B is:

$K_d(1-T) = I(1-T)/MV$
$K_d(1-T) = (\$6 \times 0.7)/\$105 = 0.04$ or 4%

Cost of redeemable debt

Investor return (k_d) can be found by calculating the internal rate of return (IRR) of the investment cash flows:

T_0	MV	(x)
T_{1-n}	Interest payments	x
T_n	Capital repayment	x

Cost of debt ($k_d(1-T)$) to the company can be found using the internal rate of return (IRR) of the investment cash flows:

T_0	MV	(x)
T_{1-n}	Interest payments × (1 – T)	x
T_n	Capital repayment	x

Remember, the internal rate of return (IRR) is the discount rate at which the net present value is zero. Use the tables provided in the exam to calculate the net present value for different discount rates.

For example,
company B has in issue 6% redeemable debt with 6 years to redemption. Redemption will be at par. The current market value of the debt is $92.96. The rate of corporation tax is 30%.

The cost of debt to the company (post-tax cost of debt) is:

time	cash flow	df/af 5%	PV	df/af 10%	PV
t0	$(92.96)	1	$(92.96)	1	$(92.96)
t1 to 6	$4.20	5.076	$21.32	4.355	$18.29
t6	$100.00	0.746	$74.60	0.564	$56.40
		NPV =	$2.96	NPV =	$(18.27)

df = discount factor, af = annuity factor (from the tables)
the cash flows for years 1 to 6 are $4.20 ($100 x 6% x 70%) (after tax)

IRR = 5 + [$2.96/($2.96 – $(18.27))] × (10 – 5)

IRR = 5 + 0.139 × 5 = 5.7%

Cost of convertible debt

- Calculate the value of the conversion option using available data.
- Compare the conversion option with the cash option. Assume all investors will choose the option with the higher value and use this as the redemption value in the calculations.
- Calculate the IRR of the flows as for redeemable debt.

Note: there is no tax effect whichever option is chosen at the conversion date.

Cost of non-tradeable debt   cost to company = interest x (1 – T)

The weighted average cost of capital (WACC)

KEY POINT Funds from each source of long-term finance are pooled together and used to finance the various investment projects. Therefore, a weighted average cost of these sources of finance is appropriate to evaluate the investment projects.

The formula is given in the exam.

The WACC calculation:

Calculate weights for each source of capital.

Estimate the cost of each source of capital.

Multiply proportion of total of each source by its cost and sum the results, using the formula:

$$\text{WACC} = \left(\frac{V_e}{V_e + V_d} \right) k_e + \left(\frac{V_d}{V_e + V_d} \right) k_d(1-T)$$

V_e and V_d are the market values of equity and of debt.

Do you understand?

1   Company F has 10 million 35c ordinary shares in issue with a current price of 175c cum-div. An annual dividend of 10c has been proposed. Annual dividends have been growing at a steady rate of 4% per annum. The company's other major source of funds is $2 million 8% irredeemable loan notes with a market value of $120 per $100 par value.

If the company pays corporation tax at a rate of 30%, what is the weighted average cost of capital (WACC) that should be used for assessing projects, rounded to one decimal place?

A   9.6%

B   9.7%

C   9.9%

D   10.0%

---

1   A. Cost of equity = 0.1 (1.04)/(1.75 – 0.1) + 0.04 = 10.3%. Post tax cost of debt = 8 (1 – 0.30) × 100 /120 = 4.7%. WACC = (10.3% × 16.5/18.9) + (4.7% × 2.4/18.9) = 9.6%. NB. 16.5 (10 × (1.75 – 0.10), 2.4 (2 × 1.2), 18.9 (16.5 + 2.4).

The impact of risk

KEY POINT The total return demanded by an investor is dependent on two specific factors, which are the prevailing risk-free rate (R_f) of return, and the reward investors demand for the risk they take in advancing funds to the firm.

DEFINITION The **risk-free rate (R_f)** is the minimum rate required by all investors for an investment whose returns are certain.

Return on risky investments – loan notes	Loan notes are riskier than government gilts.
	They are less risky than equity investment because:
	interest is a legal commitment
	interest will be paid before any dividends
	loans are often secured.
	Returns on loan notes will be higher than R_f but lower than on equities.
Return on risky investments – equities	The return required by equity investors can be shown as:
	required return = risk-free return + risk premium.

17.2 THE CAPITAL ASSET PRICING MODEL

LEARNING SUMMARY

After studying this section you should be able to:

- discuss the relationship between portfolio theory and the capital asset pricing model

- estimate the cost of equity using the capital asset pricing model.

KEY POINT The capital asset pricing model (CAPM) enables us to calculate the required return from an investment given the level of risk associated with the investment (measured by its beta factor).

In order to explain how the CAPM works, it is first necessary to introduce the concepts of systematic and unsystematic risk:

Systematic risk ····▶ caused by general, macro-economic factors (e.g. recession, interest rates, exchange rates).

Unsystematic risk ····▶ caused by factors specific to the company or industry (e.g. systems failure, research and development success, strikes).

- As an investor increases the size of his portfolio, overall risk reduces.

- Systematic risk cannot be eliminated by diversification.

The theory of CAPM

The CAPM gives a required return for a given level of systematic risk.

Therefore, if we can estimate the level of risk associated with an entity (the beta of the entity), we can use CAPM to give a required return to shareholders.

This required return to shareholders is essentially the cost of equity which can then be used to derive an appropriate WACC for the entity.

The formula is given in the exam.

The CAPM formula and the beta factor

$$E(r_j) = R_f + \beta_i[E(r_m) - R_f]$$

β_i = the entity's 'beta factor' – a measure of the **systematic** risk of investment i relative to the market

note - it is assumed that investors are well diversified

$E(r_j)$ = required rate of return of the investor (equivalent to k_e)

R_f = risk-free rate of return

$E(r_m)$ = expected average return on the market (shortened to R_m)

$E(r_m) - R_f$ = equity risk premium

For example,
the current average market return being paid on risky investments is 15%, compared with 7% on government gilts. Company E has a beta figure of 0.9.

The required return of an equity investor in company E is:

$E(r_j) = R_f + \beta_i[E(r_m) - R_f]$

$E(r_j) = 7 + 0.9 \times (15 - 7)$

$E(r_j) = 14.2\%$

Assumptions of the CAPM are:

Well diversified investors – who only need to be compensated for systematic risk.

Perfect capital market – no taxes, no transaction costs, perfect information, etc.

Unrestricted borrowing/lending at the risk-free rate.

Single period transaction horizon – usually one year.

An efficient market where it is possible to diversify away unsystematic risk, and no transaction costs.

Do you understand?

1   Risk that cannot be diversified away can be described as:

   A   Systematic risk

   B   Financial risk

   C   Unsystematic risk

   D   Business risk

1. A.

Exam style questions

1   The equity shares of a company have a beta value of 0.80. The risk-free rate of return is 6% and the market risk premium is 4%. Corporation tax is 30%.

   What is the required return on the shares of the company (to one decimal place)?

2   A company has just declared an ordinary dividend of 25.6p per share; the cum-div market price of an ordinary share is 280p.

   Assuming a dividend growth rate of 16% per annum, what is the company's cost of equity capital (to one decimal place)?

3   Company J's capital structure is as follows:

	$m
50c ordinary shares	12
8% $1 preference shares	6
12.5% loan notes 20X6	8
	26

   The loan notes are redeemable at nominal value in 20X7. The current market prices of the company's securities are as follows.

50c ordinary shares	250c
8% $1 preference shares	92c
12.5% loan notes 20X6	$100

   The company is paying corporation tax at the rate of 30%. The cost of the company's ordinary equity capital has been estimated at 18% pa.

   What is the company's weighted average cost of capital for capital investment appraisal purposes?

   A   9.71%

   B   13.53%

   C   16.29%

   D   16.73%

18 Capital structure

The following topics are covered in this chapter:
- Gearing
- Capital structure theories

18.1 GEARING

LEARNING SUMMARY

After studying this section you should be able to:

- describe the traditional view of capital structure and its assumptions.

Operating gearing
a measure of the extent to which a firm's operating costs are fixed rather than variable

$$= \frac{\text{Fixed costs}}{\text{Variable costs}}$$

or

$$= \frac{\text{Fixed costs}}{\text{Total costs}}$$

or

$$= \frac{\% \text{ change in EBIT}}{\% \text{ change in revenue}}$$

EBIT = earnings before interest and tax
The higher the proportion of fixed costs the higher the operating gearing and the riskier the EBIT.

Financial gearing
a measure of the extent to which debt is used in the capital

$$\text{Equity gearing} = \frac{\text{Debt}}{\text{Equity}}$$

$$\text{Total or capital gearing} = \frac{\text{Debt}}{\text{Total capital}}$$

$$\text{Interest gearing} = \frac{\text{Debt interest}}{\text{Operating profit before debt interest and tax}}$$

Can be calculated using book values or market values.
An increase in financial gearing represents an increase in risk.

Do you understand?

1 Which of the following events is most likely to lead to an increase in the firm's operating risk?

    A   An increase in the proportion of the firm's operating capital which is debt

    B   An increase in the proportion of the firm's operating costs which are fixed

    C   An increase in the proportion of the firm's operating capital which is equity

    D   An increase in the proportion of the firm's operating costs which are variable

1 B.

Market value (MV) of a company =	present value (PV) of its future cash flows discounted at the weighted average cost of capital (WACC).

As an entity increases its gearing i.e. the amount of debt in its capital
structure, two things happen to the cost of capital (WACC):

1. Debt is a cheaper source of finance than equity (lower risk and tax relief on interest) so the
WACC falls by introducing more debt.

2. The equity holders perceive more risk caused by the increase in debt, so the cost of equity
rises and hence WACC rises.

The traditional view of capital structure

The traditional view is based on real world observation:

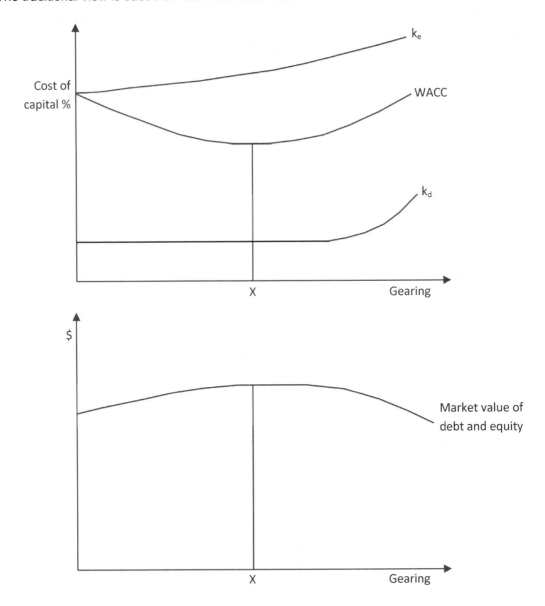

Conclusions of the traditional view:

Shareholder wealth is affected by changing the level of gearing.

There is an optimal gearing ratio at which WACC is minimised and the total value of the company is maximised.

Financial managers have a duty to achieve and maintain this ratio.

While we accept that the WACC is probably U shaped for entities generally, we cannot precisely calculate a best gearing level.

The optimal level will differ from one entity to another and can only be found by trial and error.

Do you understand?

1   According to the traditional view of capital structure, which of the following statements is incorrect?

    A   As the level of gearing increases, the cost of debt remains unchanged up to a certain level of gearing. Beyond this level, the cost of debt will increase.

    B   The cost of equity falls as the level of gearing increases and financial risk increases.

    C   The weighted average cost of capital does not remain constant, but rather falls initially as the proportion of debt capital increases, and then begins to increase as the rising cost of equity (and possibly debt) becomes more significant.

    D   The optimal level of gearing is where the company's weighted average cost of capital is minimised.

1. B.

18.2 CAPITAL STRUCTURE THEORIES

LEARNING SUMMARY

After studying this section you should be able to:

- describe the views of Miller and Modigliani on capital structure

- identify and discuss the problems of high levels of gearing

- explain the relevance of pecking order theory to the selection of sources of finance

- understand the capital asset pricing model and gearing risk.

Modigliani and Miller (M&M) – 1958 theory with no taxation

M & M's key assumptions:

There exists a perfect capital market in which there are no information costs or transaction costs.

Debt is risk free and k_d remains constant at all levels of gearing.

There is no taxation.

M & M's no tax theory - in the absence of tax, gearing levels have no impact on WACC or company value:

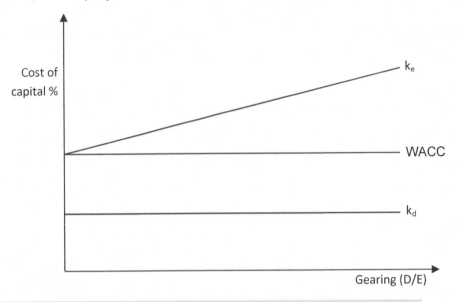

Modigliani and Miller (M&M) – 1963 theory with taxation

When the effect of tax is taken into account, the tax relief on debt interest causes the WACC to fall (and the business value to rise) as gearing increases.

The implication is - the optimum gearing level is 99.9% debt.

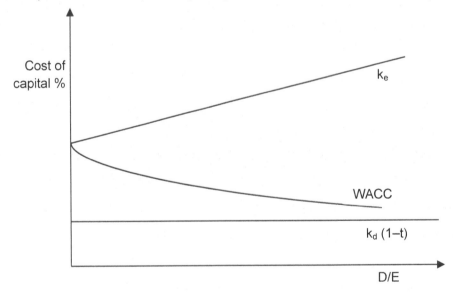

The problems of high gearing

Businesses are rarely found with very high levels of gearing due to:

Bankruptcy risk	increased cash commitments on interest and redemption payments can reduce cash balances.
Agency costs	restrictions by existing lenders on management actions.
Tax exhaustion	no tax liability left against which to offset interest charges.
The impact on borrowing/debt capacity	no further assets on which to secure debt reduces lenders' willingness to lend.
Difference between risk tolerance levels between directors and shareholders	management's unwillingness to take risks that well diversified investors would accept.
Restrictions in the articles of association	which can specify borrowing limits.
Increase in the cost of borrowing as gearing increases	due to bankruptcy risk and lack of assets for security.

Pecking-order theory

In this theory, there is no search for an optimal capital structure through a theorised process. Instead it is argued that businesses will raise new funds as follows:

internally generated funds - already available, cheap

debt - less contentious than share issues, moderate issue costs

new issue of equity - could be perceived as a sign of problems, expensive.

Do you understand?

1   M & M stated that, in the absence of tax, a company's capital structure would have no impact on its weighted average cost of capital.

Which of the following are their assumptions?

(1)   A perfect capital market exists, in which investors have the same information, upon which they act rationally.

(2)   There are no tax or transaction costs.

(3)   Debt is risk-free and freely available at the same cost to investors and companies alike.

A   (2) only

B   (1) and (2) only

C   (1) and (3) only

D   all of the above

Capital structure and the choice of discount rate

KEY POINT If an investment significantly changes the proportions of debt and equity or the risk levels of the firm, or the finance is project-specific, then the existing WACC will no longer be an appropriate rate at which to discount the investment cash flows.

When it is the risk that has changed (either by altering the gearing levels or by moving into a different business area) the capital asset pricing model (CAPM) may be used to find an up to date cost of equity to be used in a new calculation of the WACC.

CAPM and gearing risk

The CAPM uses a beta factor to represent the systematic risk levels of the investment.

There are two types of beta factor:

Asset beta (β_a)
- the beta for an ungeared company
- represents the systematic risk of the business type only (business risk)

Equity beta (β_e)
- the beta for a geared company
- represents both the business risk and the financial risk (related to gearing levels) of the company

KEY POINT To use the CAPM to find a cost of equity for use in investment appraisal, a beta with both the correct business risk (for the investment type) and the correct financial risk (for the company undertaking the investment) must be determined.

The formula is given in the exam.

Steps to calculate a discount rate for use in investment appraisal:

Find an appropriate asset beta that reflects the correct business risk for the project – this may involve de-gearing a proxy equity beta using the formula:

$$\beta_a = \left[\frac{V_e}{V_e + V_d(1-T)} \right] \beta_e + \left[\frac{V_d}{V_e + V_d(1-T)} \right] \beta_d$$

Note - β_d will be assumed to be zero.

V_e and V_d are the market values of equity and debt of the proxy company.

If more than one proxy asset beta is provided, use an average figure.

Re-gear the asset beta to reflect the gearing levels of the company making the investment (use the same formula but this time to find β_e from β_a using the market values of equity and debt for the investing company).

Use the re-geared beta to find the risk-adjusted cost of equity using the CAPM.

If a WACC is needed, use the new cost of equity in the WACC calculation (calculation outside the scope of the syllabus).

Do you understand?

1   Two companies are identical in every respect except for their capital structure.
Company X has a debt to equity ratio of 1:3 and an equity beta of 1.2. Company Y has a
debt to equity ratio of 2:3. Corporation tax is 30%.

What is an appropriate equity beta for Company Y?

A   0.93

B   1.43

C   1.62

D   1.76

1   **Which of the following would be implied by a decrease in a company's operating gearing ratio?**

A   The company is less profitable

B   The company is more risky

C   The company has a lower proportion of costs that are variable

D   The company has profits which are less sensitive to changes in sales volume

2   **Which of the following statements is part of the traditional theory of gearing?**

A   There must be taxes

B   There must exist a minimum WACC

C   Cost of debt increases as gearing decreases

D   Cost of equity increases as gearing decreases

3   **If a geared company's asset beta is used in the CAPM formula ($r_j = r_f + \beta_j (r_m - r_f)$) what will r_j represent?**

A   The WACC of the company

B   The ungeared cost of equity

C   The geared cost of equity

D   The market premium

19.1 RATIO ANALYSIS

LEARNING SUMMARY

After studying this section you should be able to:

* describe and apply ways of measuring the achievement of corporate objectives through ratio analysis.

KEY POINT Ratio analysis is the process of comparing and quantifying relationships between financial variables, such as those variables found in the statement of financial position and statement of profit or loss of a company.

Ratios can assist with:

measuring the achievement of corporate objectives	capital structure
investment appraisal	business valuations
working capital management	

Profitability and return ratios

Return on capital employed (ROCE)
a measure of how efficiently a business is using the funds available, it measures how much is earned per $1 invested

$$= \frac{\text{Profit before interest and tax}}{\text{Capital employed}} \times 100$$

capital employed =
total assets – current liabilities, or
total equity + long term debt

Return on equity (ROE)
a measure of how much profit a company generates for its ordinary shareholders with the money they have invested in the company

$$= \frac{\text{Profit after tax and preference dividends}}{\text{Ordinary share capital and reserves}} \times 100$$

Profit margins
measure how well revenue is converted into profit by the company.

$$= \frac{\text{Profit}}{\text{Revenue}} \times 100$$

Debt and gearing ratios

Interest cover
a measure of the adequacy of a company's profits relative to its interest payments on its debt

$$= \frac{\text{Operating profit before interest and tax}}{\text{Debt interest}} \times 100$$

See chapter 18 for the gearing ratios.

Investor ratios

Earnings per share (EPS)
the basic measure of a company's performance from an ordinary shareholder's point of view - it is the amount of profit attributable to each ordinary share

$$= \frac{\text{Profit after interest, tax and preference share dividends}}{\text{Number of ordinary shares in issue}}$$

Price/Earnings (PE) ratio
a basic measure of company performance, it expresses the amount the shareholders are prepared to pay for the share as a multiple of current earnings

$$= \frac{\text{Share price}}{\text{Earnings per share (EPS)}}$$

Dividend per share (DPS)
helps individual ordinary shareholders see how much of the overall dividend pay-out they are entitled to

$$= \frac{\text{Total dividend}}{\text{Total number of shares issued}}$$

Dividend cover
a measure of how many times the company's earnings could pay the dividend

$$= \frac{\text{Profit available for ordinary shareholders}}{\text{Dividend for the year}}$$

Dividend yield
a direct measure of the wealth received by the ordinary shareholder

$$= \frac{\text{Dividend per share (DPS)}}{\text{Market price per share}} \times 100$$

| Total shareholder return (TSR)
a measure of the income to the investor by taking account of capital growth and dividend income | ┄┄┄► | = | $\dfrac{\text{Dividend per share (DPS) + change in share price}}{\text{Share price at the start of the period}} \times 100$ |

| Interest yield
a measure of the interest on debt expressed as a percentage of the market price | ┄┄┄► | = | $\dfrac{\text{Interest}}{\text{Market value of debt}} \times 100$ |

Do you understand?

1   In the year to 30 September 20X7, an advertising agency declares an interim ordinary dividend of 7.4c per share, and a final ordinary dividend of 8.6c per share.

Assuming an ex-div share price of 315c, what is the dividend yield?

A   2.35%

B   2.73%

C   5.08%

D   4.10%

2   The price/earnings (PE) ratio:

A   measures how much profits a company generates for its ordinary shareholders with the money they have invested in the company

B   is a basic measure of the amount of profit attributable to each ordinary share

C   expresses the amount the shareholders are prepared to pay for the shares as a multiple of current earnings

D   helps individual ordinary shareholders see how much of the overall dividend pay-out they are entitled to

1. C. ((7.4 + 8.6)/315).
2. C.

1   **Which TWO of the following statements concerning profit are correct?**

    1   Accounting profit is not the same as economic profit

    2   Profit takes account of risk

    3   Accounting profit can be manipulated by managers

    4   Gross profit margin is calculated as gross profit divided by shareholder's funds

2   **Which of the following ratios is used to measure a company's liquidity?**

    A   Current ratio

    B   Interest cover

    C   Gross profit margin

    D   Return on capital employed

3   **What is the dividend cover ratio a measure of?**

    A   How many times the company's earnings could pay the dividend

    B   The interest or coupon rate expressed as a percentage of the market price

    C   The returns to the investor by taking about of dividend income and capital growth

    D   How much of the overall dividend pay-out the individual shareholders are entitled to

20 Business valuations

The following topics are covered in this chapter:
- Valuing business and financial assets
- Models for the valuation of shares
- The valuation of debt
- Market efficiency and the efficient market hypothesis

20.1 VALUING BUSINESS AND FINANCIAL ASSETS

LEARNING SUMMARY

After studying this section you should be able to:

- identify and discuss reasons for valuing businesses and financial assets.

Valuations of shares in both public and private companies are needed for several purposes by investors including:

to establish terms of takeovers and mergers

to be able to make 'buy and hold' decisions

to value companies entering the stock market

to establish values of shares held by retiring directors

for fiscal purposes (such as, capital gains tax and inheritance tax)

for other reasons, such as divorce settlements.

There are three main approaches to valuations:

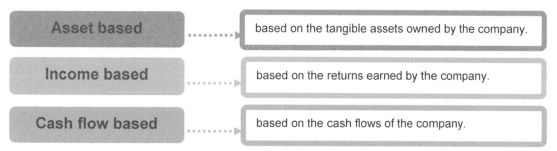

Asset based	based on the tangible assets owned by the company.
Income based	based on the returns earned by the company.
Cash flow based	based on the cash flows of the company.

Market capitalisation

KEY POINT The market capitalisation of a public company is found by multiplying its current share price by the number of shares in issue.

- Share prices of companies on the stock exchange move constantly, and therefore so do their market capitalisations.

- The values calculated in this way do not necessarily reflect the actual market value of companies, as a premium may be paid to purchase, for example, a controlling interest.

Real worth of a company

KEY POINT Ultimately the real worth of a company will only be known once a purchase has been made after negotiation between the two parties.

20.2 MODELS FOR THE VALUATION OF SHARES

LEARNING SUMMARY

After studying this section you should be able to:

- understand and apply asset based valuation models

- understand and apply income based valuation models

- understand and apply cash flow based valuation models.

Asset based valuations

KEY POINT Asset based valuations involve adding up the value of the company's assets and deducting the value of any purchased liabilities.

Types of asset based measures:

Measure	Strengths	Weaknesses
Book value	relatively easy to obtain	uses the historic cost
Replacement value	maximum to be paid for assets by the buyer	ignores goodwill similar assets may not exist
Breakup value/net realisable value	minimum amount acceptable to the owners	ignores goodwill may be difficult to value

- Asset based valuations do not value what is being purchased, i.e. the right to future earnings/cash flows of the company.

- They also ignore intangible assets, such as goodwill, which are particularly relevant for service companies, which may have skilled workers, strong management, or a strong customer base relative to its competitors.

Do you understand?

1   An independent accountant has produced the following valuations of a private company:

Historical cost adjusted for changes in general purchasing power	$3.2m
Piecemeal net realisable value	$4.1m
Cost of setting up an equivalent venture	$5.3m
Economic value of the business	$5.6m

Assuming that the above valuations accord with the expectations and risk perceptions of the purchaser, what is the maximum price that should be paid for the company?

A $3.2m

B $4.1m

C $5.3m

D $5.6m

1. C.

Income based valuations

Price/Earnings (PE) ratio method

Value per share =
earnings per share (EPS) × PE ratio

Total value of equity =
total earnings × PE ratio

The starting point is the current post tax earnings, after the preference share dividends, but before ordinary dividends.

Adjust for one-off factors, such as:
- one-off items which will not recur in the coming year (e.g. debt write offs in the previous year)
- directors' salaries which might be adjusted after a takeover has been completed
- synergies, two or more businesses can work together to achieve more than the sum of their individual efforts.

Earnings yield method

Value per share =
EPS × 1/earnings yield

Total value of equity =
total earnings × 1/earnings yield

Incorporating constant growth (g) in earnings:

Total value of equity =
earnings x (1 + g)/earnings yield - g

The earnings yield is the inverse of the PE ratio.

For example,
Company J has earnings of $1.2 million. A similar listed company has an earnings yield of 11%. J's earnings have been growing at a rate of 2% per annum but it is unknown as to whether this will continue.
The value of Company J if growth is maintained at 2% per annum is:

Value = ($1.2m × 1.02)/(0.11 − 0.02) = $13.6 million.

Cash flow based valuations – the dividend valuation model (DVM)

The value of the company/share is the present value (PV) of the expected future dividends, discounted at the shareholder's required rate of return:

The method

$$P_0 = \frac{D}{r_e} \quad \text{or}$$

$$P_0 = \frac{D_0 (1 + g)}{r_e - g}$$

P_0 = value of company
D = total dividend
r_e = shareholder's required return
g = annual growth rate

The second formula is given in the exam.

r_e will be given in the question or may be calculated using the capital asset pricing model.

For example,
A company has the following information available:

Share capital in issue: 2 million ordinary shares at a par value of $0.75.
Dividend just paid: $0.10 per share.
Dividend 5 years ago: $0.07 per share.
Current equity beta: 0.9.
Average market return on shares: 16%.
Risk free rate: 7%.

The market capitalisation of the company is:
Market capitalisation = number of shares in issue × market price per share.
$P_0 = D_0(1 + g)/(k_e - g)$
$K_e = R_f + \beta(R_m - R_f)$
$K_e = 7 + 0.9 \times (16 - 7) = 15.1\%$
$g = (D_0/D_n)^{1/n} - 1$
$g = (0.1/0.07)^{1/5} - 1 = 0.0739$ or 7.4%
$P_0 = (\$0.10 \times 1.074)/(0.151 - 0.074) = \$1.39$ per share
Market capitalisation = $1.39 × 2m = $2.78m.

The model is theoretically sound and good for valuing a non-controlling interest, but:

- There may be problems estimating a future growth rate.

- Growth is assumed to be zero or at a constant rate.

- The model is highly sensitive to changes in its assumptions.

- There are few advantages over earnings based methods for controlling interests.

The discounted cash flow basis

The steps for valuation are:

Identify the free cash flows	operating cash flows excluding financing flows
	deduct tax cash flows
	add revenue from sale of assets
	add cash flow benefit of synergies from the merger
	deduct the cash flow for ongoing asset expenditure, e.g. replacement of worn out fixed assets.
Select a suitable time horizon.	
Calculate the present value (PV) over this time period	this gives the total value to all providers of finance, i.e. equity and debt.
If valuing equity only, deduct the value of the debt	which is now a liability for the new owner, to give the equity value.

The strengths and weaknesses of the discounted cash flow method are:

Strengths	Weaknesses
Theoretically the best method, as the PV of the future cash flows represents the shareholder wealth increase.	Relies on estimates of cash flows and discount rates.
Can be used to value all or part of a company.	Difficulty in choosing a time horizon.
	Difficulty in valuing a company's worth beyond this time horizon.
	Assumes that discount rates, tax and inflation rates are constant over the period.

Valuation post-takeover

In this situation, when estimating the effect of the takeover on the total value of the company, and on the value per share, it is important to take into account:

- Synergy - which adds value to the combined entity.

- Method of financing - cash reduces value, share for share reduces value per share.

20.3 THE VALUATION OF DEBT

LEARNING SUMMARY

After studying this section you should be able to:

- apply appropriate valuation methods to irredeemable debt, redeemable debt, convertible debt and preference shares.

The valuation of debt uses the same principles seen in the cost of capital chapter (17), with the calculations rearranged.

Preference shares	$P_0 = D/K_p$	D = constant dividend from year 1 to infinity
		P_0 = ex div market price of a share
		K_p = cost of the preference share
Irredeemable debt	$MV = I/r$	I = annual interest starting in one year's time
		MV = ex-interest market price of the loan note
		r = debt holders' required return, expressed as a decimal
Redeemable debt	PV of future interest and redemption receipts (or value of converted shares if convertible debt) discounted at investors' required return rate	PV = present value

Do you understand?

1   A firm has issued irredeemable loan notes with a coupon rate of 7%.

If the required return of investors is 4%, the current market value of the debt is $100.

True or False

1   False. The current market value is $175 (7/0.04).

20.4 MARKET EFFICIENCY AND THE EFFICIENT MARKET HYPOTHESIS

LEARNING SUMMARY

After studying this section you should be able to:

- distinguish between and discuss weak form efficiency, semi-strong efficiency and strong form efficiency

- discuss practical considerations in the valuation of shares and businesses.

The concept of market efficiency

DEFINITION   An **efficient market** is one in which security prices fully reflect all available information (i.e. they are fairly priced).

- In an efficient market, new information is rapidly and rationally incorporated into share prices in an unbiased way.

- Fairly priced shares ensure investor confidence and reflect director performance.

The efficient market hypothesis

There are three forms of efficiency based on different theories about where this new information comes from:

Weak form efficiency
In a weak form efficient market share prices reflect information about all past price movements. Past movements do not help investors in identifying positive NPV trading strategies.

Share prices follow a random walk:
- There are no patterns or trends.
- Prices rise or fall depending on whether the next piece of news is good or bad.
- Very little of a share price movement on one day can be predicted from knowledge of the change on the previous day.

Conclusion for the stock market:
- Future price movements cannot be predicted from past price movements.
- Chartism/technical analysis cannot help make consistent gains on the market.

Semi-strong form efficiency
In a semi-strong form efficient market share prices incorporate all past information and all publicly-available information. Semi-strong market efficiency incorporates weak form market efficiency.

Share prices react within 5 – 10 minutes of any new information being released:
- Rising in response to good news.
- Falling in response to bad news.

Conclusion for the stock market:
- Fundamental analysis – examining publicly-available information will not provide opportunities to consistently beat the market.
- Only those trading in the first few minutes after the news breaks can beat the market.

Strong form efficiency
In a strongly efficient market share prices incorporate all information, whether public or private, including information which is as yet unpublished.

Insiders (directors, for example) have access to unpublished information. If the market was strong form:
- Share prices would not move with breaking news as they would have already reacted before the news became public.
- There would be no need to ban 'insider dealing' as insiders would not be able to beat the market.

Conclusion for the stock market:
- Insider dealing is banned.
- The stock exchange encourages the release of new information quickly to prevent insider dealing opportunities.
- Insiders are forbidden from dealing in their shares at crucial times.

Practical considerations in the valuation of shares and businesses

- Marketability and liquidity of shares - unquoted company shares are often worth less than similar quoted ones as they are unlikely to be easily sold.

- Available information - may be less readily available for unlisted companies.

- Equilibrium prices - share prices in reality can be more volatile than expected from the market efficiency theory. Prices that are not in equilibrium should be treated with caution.

Do you understand?

1 An investor who bases all his investment decisions solely on an analysis of past share price movements is acting as if he believes that the capital market is:

A   Strongly efficient

B   Semi-strongly efficient

C   Weakly efficient

D   Not efficient at any level

1 D.

Exam style questions

Recent financial information relating to Company C, a stock market listed company, is as follows.

	$m
Profit after tax (earnings)	66.6
Dividends	40.0

Statement of financial position information:

	$m	$m
Non-current assets		595
Current assets		125
Total assets		720
Current liabilities		70
Equity		
Ordinary shares ($1 nominal)	80	
Reserves	410	
		490
Non-current liabilities		
6% Bank loan	40	
8% Bonds ($100 nominal)	120	
		160
		720

Financial analysts have forecast that the dividends of Company C will grow in the future at a rate of 4% per year. This is slightly less than the forecast growth rate of the profit after tax (earnings) of the company, which is 5% per year. The finance director of Company C thinks that, considering the risk associated with expected earnings growth, an earnings yield of 11% per year can be used for valuation purposes.

Company C has a cost of equity of 10% per year and a before-tax cost of debt of 7% per year. The 8% bonds will be redeemed at nominal value in six years' time. Company C pays tax at an annual rate of 30% per year and the ex-dividend share price of the company is $8.50 per share.

Required:

1   Calculate the value of Company C using the following methods:

   (a)   net asset value method

   (b)   dividend growth model

   (c)   earnings yield method.

2   Calculate the weighted average after-tax cost of capital of Company C using market values where appropriate.

3   Discuss the circumstances under which the weighted average cost of capital (WACC) can be used as a discount rate in investment appraisal. Briefly indicate alternative approaches that could be adopted when using the WACC is not appropriate.

CHAPTER 1

1   C

The others are secondary objectives that could be used to help achieve the primary objective.

2   Statements 2, 3 and 5 are financial objectives

Achieving market share (a relative measure), or customer satisfaction (a qualitative measure), are non-financial objectives.

3   All three statements are true

4   C

5   A, B and D

Managerial reward schemes should be clearly defined and impossible to manipulate.

CHAPTER 2

1   B

$8,000 + $40,000 + $25,000. Depreciation is a non cash item and the fixed costs would be incurred anyway, therefore they are both added back.

2   (a)   A

Cumulative cash flows are $(2,700,000) at the end of year 1, $(1,200,000) at the end of year 2 and $400,000 at the end of year 3. Therefore 2 years + ($1,200,000 ÷ $1,600,000) = 2.75 years.

(b)   B

Average annual accounting profit = ((Total operating cash flows – total depreciation) ÷ life of project) = ($5,880,000 – $3,800,000) ÷ 4 = $520,000 per year

Average investment = ($3,900,000 + $100,000) ÷2 = $2,000,000

ROCE = $520,000 ÷ $2,000,000 = 26%

CHAPTER 3

1   C

In general, it is possible for a project to have up to as many IRRs as there are sign changes in the cash flows. Since the project's cash flows have two sign changes there can be up to two IRRs. The NPV profile could take various forms depending on the relative magnitudes of the cash flows.

2 **Payback period: decrease** **Internal rate of return: increase**

The payback period will decrease and the IRR increase, because the outflow at time 0 is unaffected by inflation.

3 **A**

Net initial investment = $732,000

The IRR is the interest rate at which the NPV of the investment is zero.

PV of perpetuity = $146,400/r

The IRR is where $146,400/r = $732,000

IRR = $146,400/$732,000 × 100% = 20%

If you selected 25% you in fact assumed that the first inflow is coterminous with the initial investment. If you selected 500% you calculated the $732,000 net investment correctly but your final calculation was 'upside-down'. If you selected 400% you made both of these errors.

4 **A, B and D**

IRR is based on discounted cash flow principles. It therefore considers all of the cash flows in a project (A), does not include notional accounting costs such as depreciation (B) and it considers the time value of money (D). It is not an absolute measure of return, however, as IRR is expressed as a percentage. Two projects can have the same IRR but very different cash flows. C is therefore an incorrect statement.

CHAPTER 4

1 **C**

It is the tax saving on the tax allowable depreciation that is the relevant cash flow, not the depreciation itself. The cost of capital is used for asset replacement decisions. The after tax cost of debt would be used in a lease vs buy decision. Government restrictions on bank lending would represent hard capital rationing.

2 **A**

The investment is made on 1 January 20X775, so tax-allowable depreciation can first be set off against profits for the accounting period ended 31 December 20X7. The tax cash saving will therefore be at 31 December 20X7. i.e. time 1.

Time	Date	$	Tax saved ($)	Payment time
0	1 January 20X7	2,000,000		
1	Tax-allowable depreciation	(500,000)	@ 30% = 150,000	1
		—————		
		1,500,000		
2	31 December 20X8	(350,000)		
		—————		
		1,150,000	@ 30% = 345,000	2

Present value = ($150,000 × 0.870) + ($345,000 × 0.756) = $391,320

3 **12%**

(1 + money rate) = (1 + real rate) × (1 + inflation rate)

1.21 = (1 + real rate) × 1.08

Real rate= 12%

4 **C**

Money cost of capital = [(1.08 × 1.12) − 1] × 100 = 20.96%

Time	t0	t1	t2
	$	$	$
Outlay	(18,000)		
Labour		9,000	9,900
Salvage			5,000
			————
			14,900
			————
20.96% discount factor	1	0.8267	0.6835
Present value	(18,000)	7,440	10,184

NPV = $(376) or $(380) to nearest $10

5 **C**

The NPV impact of the initial outflow is unaffected.

The revenue flows will be subject to inflation, but then should be discounted at a money rate which includes this inflation. The net effect is no change in the PV.

The sales proceeds represent a flow of money, not affected by inflation, but this will now be discounted at a higher money rate, lowering the net present value of the project.

CHAPTER 5

1 **B**

	A	B	C	D
NPV/$ of capital in restricted period	60/20	40/10	80/30	80/40
	= 3	= 4	= 2.67	= 2

The optimal sequence is BACD

2 **C**

	$	Discount factor	$
Time 0	(10,000)	1.000	(10,000)
Time 1	(3,000)	0.909	(2,727)
Time 2	(5,000)	0.826	(4,130)
Time 3	(5,000)	0.751	(3,755)
NPV			(20,612)

Equivalent annual cost = 20,612/2.487 = $8,288

3   B

	Capital needed at time 0	NPV	NPV/£ needed at time 0	Rank	Invested	NPV
	$	$	$		$	$
Project 5	10,000	30,000	3.0	2	10,000	30,000
Project 6	8,000	25,000	3.125	1	8,000	25,000
Project 7	12,000	30,000	2.5	3	12,000	30,000
Project 8	16,000	36,000	2.25	4 (1/8)	2,000	4,500
					32,000	89,500

4   D

Under a long-term lease, the lessee is responsible for repairs and maintenance of the leased asset.

CHAPTER 6

1   Calculation of net present value (NPV)

Year	1	2	3	4	5	6
	$000	$000	$000	$000	$000	$000
Sales revenue	1,600	1,600	1,600	1,600	1,600	
Variable costs	(1,100)	(1,100)	(1,100)	(1,100)	(1,100)	
Contribution	500	500	500	500	500	
Fixed costs	(160)	(160)	(160)	(160)	(160)	
Taxable cash flow	340	340	340	340	340	
Tax liabilities		(102)	(102)	(102)	(102)	(102)
After-tax cash flow	340	238	238	238	238	(102)
Working capital					90	
Scrap value					40	
Net cash flow	340	238	238	238	368	(102)
Discount factors	0.901	0.812	0.731	0.659	0.593	0.535
Present values	306	193	174	157	218	(55)

	$000
Present value of cash inflows	993
Working capital investment	(90)
Cost of machine	(800)
NPV	103

Since the investment has a positive NPV, it is financially acceptable.

2　Calculation of internal rate of return (IRR)

NPV at 11% was found to be $103,000

Year	1	2	3	4	5	6
NPV at 17%:	$000	$000	$000	$000	$000	$000
Net cash flow	340	238	238	238	368	(102)
Discount factors	0.855	0.731	0.624	0.534	0.456	0.390
Present values	291	174	149	127	168	(40)

	$000
Present value of cash inflows	869
Working capital investment	(90)
Cost of machine	(800)
NPV	(21)

IRR = 11 + (((17 – 11) × 103,000/(103,000 + 21,000)) = 11+ 5.0 = 16.0%

Since the internal rate of return of the investment (16%) is greater than the cost of capital of Company J, the investment is financially acceptable.

3　Sensitivity

Sensitivity analysis indicates which project variable is the key or critical variable, i.e. the variable where the smallest relative change makes the net present value (NPV) zero. Sensitivity analysis can show where management should focus attention in order to make an investment project successful, or where underlying assumptions should be checked for robustness.

The sensitivity of an investment project to a change in a given project variable can be calculated as the ratio of the NPV to the present value (PV) of the project variable. This gives directly the relative change in the variable needed to make the NPV of the project zero.

4　Selling price sensitivity

The PV of sales revenue = 100,000 × 16 × 3.696 = $5,913,600

The tax liability associated with sales revenue needs be considered, as the NPV is on an after-tax basis.

Tax liability arising from sales revenue = 100,000 × 16 × 0.3 = $480,000 per year

The PV of the tax liability without lagging = 480,000 × 3.696 = $1,774,080

(Alternatively, PV of tax liability without lagging = 5,913,600 × 0.3 = $1,774,080)

Lagging by one year, PV of tax liability = 1,774,080 × 0.901 = $1,598,446 After-tax PV of sales revenue = 5,913,600 – 1,598,446 = $4,315,154

Sensitivity = 100 × 103,000/4,315,154 = 2.4%

Discount rate sensitivity

The breakeven discount rate is the IRR calculated in part (b).

Increase in discount rate needed to make NPV zero = 16 – 11 = 5%

Relative change in discount rate needed to make NPV zero = 100 × 5/11 = 45%

Conclusion

Of the two variables, the key or critical variable is selling price, since the investment is more sensitive to a change in this variable (2.4%) than it is to a change in discount rate (45%).

CHAPTER 7

1   All three statements are correct

2   D

Taking longer to pay trade payables would shorten the cash cycle as cash stays with company possession for a longer period of time. Lower net operating cash flows and slower inventory turnovers are signs of a lengthening cash cycle. Depreciation expenditure is a non-cash item and does not affect the cash cycle.

3   17 weeks

	Weeks
Raw materials	6
Payables	(7)
Production	2
Finished goods	6
Receivables	10
	17

4   Current ratio: decrease   Quick ratio: increase

The current liabilities figures used as the denominator will stay the same in both cases. The total of the current assets will decrease because the reduction in the inventory value will be greater than the increase in cash. Therefore the current ratio will decrease. The total of the liquid assets will increase because of the higher cash balance. Therefore, the quick ratio will increase.

CHAPTER 8

1   C

A Just in Time inventory control system aim to reduce capital tied up in inventory, not increase it (A). The system aims to create a flexible production process which is responsive to the customer's requirements, not an inflexible process (B). With a Just in Time system, although inventory holding costs are close to zero, inventory ordering costs are high, not low as more frequent small deliveries of supplies will be needed (D).

CHAPTER 9

1   **A**

The cash operating cycle = receivables days + inventory holding period – payables days.

The receivables days = 365/average receivables turnover or 365/10.5 = 34.76. The inventory holding period = 365/inventory turnover or 365/4 = 91.25. The payables days = 365/payables turnover ratio = 365/8 = 45.63.

Putting it all together: cash operating cycle = 34.76 + 91.25 – 45.63 = 80.38.

2   **A, B and C**

Delaying payments to obtain a 'free' source of finance would be a key aspect of a company's accounts payable policy, not accounts receivable.

3   **A**

Customer bargaining power increasing is associated with increased receivables days, not payables days.

CHAPTER 10

1   **C**

Baumol tranche size = $\sqrt{(2 \times \$500 \times \$1,000,000 \div 0.05)}$ = $141,421

2   **D**

Miller-Orr spread = $3 \times (\frac{3}{4} \times \$7,000^2 \times \$500 \div (0.05/365))^{1/3}$ = $153,569

3   **A**

Month	3	4	5	6	7
Sales volume (000s)	10	11	13	16	20
Sales revenue ($000)	240	264	312	384	480
Cash sales (20%)	48.0	52.8	62.4	76.8	96
Receivables:					
1-month (25% of 80%)	–	48.0	52.8	62.4	76.8
2-month (50% of 80%)	–	–	96.0	105.6	124.8
3-month (25% of 80%)	–	–	–	48.0	52.8
				211.2	

4   **A**

CHAPTER 11

1   B

Fiscal policy is implemented through the raising and lowering of taxes and through the raising and lowering of government spending. 1 only is not correct because there is another aspect to fiscal policy other than just taxation. 2 and 3 is not correct because government actions to raise or lower the size of the money supply is an aspect of monetary policy, not fiscal policy. 1, 2, and 3 is not correct because government actions to raise or lower the size of the money supply is an aspect of monetary policy, not fiscal policy.

2   C

Statements 1 and 3 relate to monetary policy.

3   D

Monetary policy which increases the level of domestic interest rates is likely to raise exchange rates as capital is attracted into the country (statement1). Any restrictions on the stock of money, or restrictions on credit, will raise the cost of borrowing, making fewer investment projects worthwhile and discouraging expansion by companies (statement 2). Periods of credit control and high interest rates reduce consumer demand (statement 3). Monetary policy is often used to control inflation (statement 4).

4   Both statements are true

CHAPTER 12

1   Both statements are true

2   C

Money markets focus on short term financial instruments. A corporate bond is a long-term source of finance, hence is a capital market instrument.

3   A, B and D

4   A

CHAPTER 13

1   Transaction risk

This is the risk arising on short-term foreign currency transactions that the actual income or cost may be different from the income or cost expected when the transaction was agreed. For example, a sale worth $10,000 when the exchange rate is $1.79 per £ has an expected sterling value is $5,587. If the dollar has depreciated against sterling to $1.84 per £ when the transaction is settled, the sterling receipt will have fallen to $5,435. Transaction risk therefore affects cash flows and for this reason most companies choose to hedge or protect themselves against transaction risk.

Translation risk

This risk arises on consolidation of financial statements prior to reporting financial results and for this reason is also known as accounting exposure. Consider an asset worth €14 million, acquired when the exchange rate was €1.4 per $. One year later, when financial statements are being prepared, the exchange rate has moved to €1.5 per $ and the statement of financial position value of the asset has changed from $10 million to $9.3 million, resulting an unrealised (paper) loss of $0.7 million. Translation risk does not involve cash flows and so does not directly affect shareholder wealth. However, investor perception may be affected by the changing values of assets and liabilities, and so a company may choose to hedge translation risk through, for example, matching the currency of assets and liabilities (e.g. a euro-denominated asset financed by a euro-denominated loan).

Economic risk

Transaction risk is seen as the short-term manifestation of economic risk, which could be defined as the risk of the present value of a company's expected future cash flows being affected by exchange rate movements over time. It is difficult to measure economic risk, although its effects can be described, and it is also difficult to hedge against it.

This is a fairly straightforward question that has a good balance of discursive and mathematical elements. Parts 1 and 2 offer a chance to pick up some easy marks for simple 'learn and churn' type answers. To score well in parts 3 and 4 you need to be clear on the spot and forward rates provided to ensure you select the right ones.

2   **Forward market evaluation**

Net receipt in 1 month = $240,000 − $140,000 = $100,000

New Co needs to sell dollars at an exchange rate of 1.7829 + 0.003 = $1.7832 per £

Sterling value of net receipt = $100,000/1.7832 = £56,079

Receipt in 3 months = $300,000

New Co needs to sell dollars at an exchange rate of 1.7846 + 0.004 = $1.7850 per £

Sterling value of receipt in 3 months = $300,000/1.7850 = £168,067

3   **Evaluation of money-market hedge**

Expected receipt after 3 months = $300,000

Dollar interest rate over three months = 5.4/4 = 1.35%

Dollars to borrow now to have $300,000 liability after 3 months = 300,000/1.0135 = $296,004

Spot rate for selling dollars = 1.7820 + 0.0002 = $1.7822 per £

Sterling deposit from borrowed dollars at spot = $296,004/1.7822 = £166,089

Sterling interest rate over three months = 4.6/ 4 = 1.15%

Value in 3 months of sterling deposit = £166,089 × 1.0115 = £167,999

The forward market is marginally preferable to the money market hedge for the dollar receipt expected after 3 months.

4   A currency futures contract is a standardised contract for the buying or selling of a specified quantity of foreign currency. It is traded on a futures exchange and settlement takes place in three-monthly cycles ending in March, June, September and December, i.e. a company can buy or sell September futures, December futures and so on. The price of a currency futures contract is the exchange rate for the currencies specified in the contract.

When a currency futures contract is bought or sold, the buyer or seller is required to deposit a sum of money with the exchange, called initial margin. If losses are incurred as exchange rates and hence the prices of currency futures contracts change, the buyer or seller may be called on to deposit additional funds (variation margin) with the exchange. Equally, profits are credited to the margin account on a daily basis as the contract is 'marked to market'.

Most currency futures contracts are closed out before their settlement dates by undertaking the opposite transaction to the initial futures transaction, i.e. if buying currency futures was the initial transaction, it is closed out by selling currency futures. A gain made on the futures transactions will offset a loss made on the currency markets and vice versa.

New Co expects to receive $300,000 in three months' time and so is concerned that sterling may appreciate (strengthen) against the dollar, since this would result in a lower sterling receipt. The company can hedge the receipt using sterling futures contracts as follows. As New Co will be buying sterling in June with the dollars it receives from its customer, it will also want to sell June sterling futures contracts at the same time (or as close as possible) so that any movement in exchange rates is offset by the two opposite transactions. This means that New Co would have to buy the futures contracts now in order to be able to sell them in June.

CHAPTER 14

1   A

2   B

If you sell a futures contract you have a contract to borrow money (not lend). What you are selling is the contract to make interest payments.

3   C

4   B

CHAPTER 15

1   B

A funding gap often arises when SMEs want to expand beyond their available funds but are not yet ready for a listing on the stock market.

2   B

Value of a right = ((5m x $8 + 1.25m × $6)/6.25 m − $6) = $1.60

This represents the value of the right to buy 1 new share, but it takes 4 existing shares to get this right, so the right per existing share = $1.60/4 shares = $0.4 per share

3   Preference shares are a form of equity capital which carry higher risk from the company point of view than ordinary shares.

CHAPTER 16

1   D

2   B

CHAPTER 17

1   **9.2%**

   Return per CAPM = R_f + beta $(R_m - R_f)$

   Return = 6% + (0.80 × 4%) = 9.2%

   Note: market risk premium – $(R_m - R_f)$

2   **27.7%**

   $$\frac{25.6 \times 1.16}{280 - 25.6} + 0.16 = 27.7\%$$

3   **C**

   $$k = \frac{0.18 \times (24 \times 2.50) + (8/92) \times 6 \times 0.92 + 0.125 \times (1 - 0.30) \times 8}{24 \times 2.50 + 6 \times 0.92 + 8} = 16.29$$

CHAPTER 18

1   **D**

   Operating gearing = fixed costs divided by variable costs, so a decrease in the gearing ratio implies a lower proportion of fixed costs. Therefore, C is wrong.

2   **B**

   The traditional view is that, as an organisation introduces debt into its capital structure, the weighted average cost of capital will fall, because initially the benefit of cheap debt finance more than outweighs any increases in the cost of equity required to compensate equity holders for higher financial risk. As gearing continues to increase, equity holders will ask for progressively higher returns and eventually this increase will start to outweigh the benefit of cheap debt finance, and the weighted average cost of capital will rise.

3   **B**

   CAPM can be used to predict the cost of equity. Using an asset beta will predict the ungeared cost of equity. Using the equity beta (geared beta) will predict the geared cost of equity.

CHAPTER 19

1 **Statements 1 and 3 are correct.**

2 **A**

Interest cover measures a company's financial risk, gross profit margin measures operating profitability and return on capital employed measures how efficiently the company is using the funds available.

3 **A**

It is the interest yield which is the interest or coupon rate expressed as a percentage of the market price and this is a measure of return on investment for the debt holder (B). It is the total shareholder return ratio which measures the returns to the investor by taking account of dividend income and capital growth (C). It is the dividend per share ratio which helps individual shareholders see how much of the overall dividend pay-out they are entitled to (D).

CHAPTER 20

1 **Net asset valuation**

In the absence of any information about realisable values and replacement costs, net asset value is on a book value basis. It is the sum of non-current assets and net current assets, less long-term debt, i.e. 595 + 125 − 70 − 160 = $490 million.

Dividend growth model

$$P_0 = D_0 (1 + g) / (r_e - g)$$

Total dividends of $40 million are expected to grow at 4% per year and Company C has a cost of equity of 10%. Value of company = (40m × 1.04) / (0.1 − 0.04) = $693 million

Earnings yield method

Profit after tax (earnings) is $66.6 million and the finance director of Company C thinks that an earnings yield of 11% per year can be used for valuation purposes.

Ignoring growth, value of company = 66.6m/0.11 = $606 million

Alternatively, profit after tax (earnings) is expected to grow at an annual rate of 5% per year and earnings growth can be incorporated into the earnings yield method using the growth model. Value of company = (66.6m × 1.05) / (0.11 − 0.05) = $1,166 million

2 **Market value of equity**

Company C has 80 million shares in issue and each share is worth $8.50 per share. The market value of equity is therefore 80 × 8.50 = $680 million

Cost of equity

This is given as 10% per year.

Market value of 8% bonds

The market value of each bond will be the present value of the expected future cash flows (interest and principal) that arise from owning the bond. Annual interest is 8% per year and the bonds will be redeemed at their nominal value of $100 per bond in six years' time. The before-tax cost of debt is given as 7% per year and this is used as a discount rate.

It is important to take note of how succinctly the model answer arrives at the answers for each element of part 1 as time can easily be wasted with more long-winded approaches. Part 3 is a standalone requirement which could have been attempted first to gain some easy marks relatively quickly.

Present value of future interest = (8 × 4.767) = $38.14

Present value of future principal payment = (100 × 0.666) = $66.60

Ex interest bond value = 38.14 + 66.60 = $104.74 per bond

Market value of bonds = 120m × (104.74/100) = $125.7 million

After-tax cost of debt of 8% bonds

The before-tax cost of debt of the bonds is given as 7% per year.

After-tax cost of debt of bonds = 7 × (1 − 0.3) = 7 × 0.7 = 4.9% per year

Value of the 6% bank loan

The bank loan has no market value and so its book value of $40 million is used in calculating the weighted average cost of capital.

After-tax cost of debt of 6% bank loan

The interest rate of the bank loan can be used as its before-tax cost of debt. After-tax cost of debt of bank loan = 6 × (1 − 0.3) = 6 × 0.7 = 4.2% per year

Calculation of weighted average after-tax cost of capital (WACC)

Total value of company = 680m + 125.7m + 40m = $845.7m

After-tax WACC = [680/845.7] × 10 + [125.7/845.7] × 4.9 + [40/845.7] × 4.2 = 9.0 % per year

3   The weighted average cost of capital (WACC) is the average return required by current providers of finance. The WACC therefore reflects the current risk of a company's business operations (business risk) and way in which the company is currently financed (financial risk). When the WACC is used as discount rate to appraise an investment project, an assumption is being made that the project's business risk and financial risk are the same as those currently faced by the investing company. If this is not the case, a marginal cost of capital or a project-specific discount rate must be used to assess the acceptability of an investment project.

The business risk of an investment project will be the same as current business operations if the project is an extension of existing business operations, and if it is small in comparison with current business operations. If this is the case, existing providers of finance will not change their current required rates of return. If these conditions are not met, a project-specific discount rate should be calculated, for example by using the capital asset pricing model.

The financial risk of an investment project will be the same as the financial risk currently faced by a company if debt and equity are raised in the same proportions as currently used, thus preserving the existing capital structure. If this is the case, the current WACC can be used to appraise a new investment project. It may still be appropriate to use the current WACC as a discount rate even when the incremental finance raised does not preserve the existing capital structure, providing that the existing capital structure is preserved on an average basis over time via subsequent finance-raising decisions.

Where the capital structure is changed by finance raised for an investment project, it may be appropriate to use the marginal cost of capital rather than the WACC.

Index

Index

Index

Index